Birch Cottage, Orsett

Coppid Hall, Stifford

Royal Oak, South Ockendon

EXPLORING

Photographs by Terry Carney

South Ockendon Church

Horndon and Langdon Hills

THURROCK
- an Historical Guide
by Christopher Harrold

The Lightship, Grays Beach

Hollow Cottages, Purfleet

Text and illustrations Copyright 1994

ISBN 0 9506141 4 9

British Library Cataloguing-in-Publication Data.
A catalogue record for this book is available
from the British Library.

Published by Thurrock Council
in partnership with
Thurrock Local History Society

Civic Offices
New Road, Grays Thurrock,
Essex RM17 6SL

CONTENTS

Introduction 2

Western Approaches 5

Central Thurrock 17

The Tilburys 31

The Fenland 43

The Highlands 53

Eastern Approaches 61

Bibliography 72

Indices
    People 76
    Places 80
    Subjects/Groups............. 84

Introduction

This book aims to fill the need for an up-to-date guide to Thurrock, seen from the viewpoint of Local History. It has been written with today's motorist in mind, providing maps and following a scheme in which the reader travels from west to east across the area. In the pages which follow there are examples of the wide variety of good things which can be seen in Thurrock.

The name of the Borough was taken from the ancient parishes Little Thurrock, Grays Thurrock and West Thurrock. The name Thurrock probably derives from the Saxon "turruc", the bottom of a ship where the water collects, a reference perhaps to the Thames marshes which make up a large part of this area. A major factor in development has been the nature of the terrain - the marshland by the river, later to be reclaimed for major industrial use, and the gravel terraces, chalk outcrop and clay beds whose excavation has scarred the landscape. More recently the Metropolitan Green Belt has affected development.

Building materials are substantially wood and local brick. The number of attractive timber-framed houses and cottages and huge barns weatherboarded in elm provides ample evidence of the durability of the wood. There is no first-class local stone; nevertheless Kentish ragstone and knapped flints in parish churches, together with brick, especially in garden walls, lend character to the area. These materials make reconstruction easier and this leads to the presence of a range of architectural periods in many buildings.

I have included stories of the people who have made our history and in so doing I have chosen to pass on information which aims to be authentic rather than legendary or hearsay. The interested reader who wishes to pursue the story of Thurrock further is provided with a bibliography.

My thanks go to those too numerous to mention who have given me the benefit of their knowledge and experience. In acknowledging my debt to others I should however mention the Museum and Library staff and in particular Terry Carney, Deputy Curator, and Randal Bingley, the former Curator, who critically reviewed and made helpful suggestions for the text itself. The maps, based on the Ordnance Survey, and illustrations are the work of local artist Timothy Harrold.

We are particularly fortunate that Thurrock Local History Society, through its Chairman John Webb, and Thurrock Council, through its Arts Officer Mark Allinson, commissioned this Guide as a contribution to the growing interest in Local History in the area.

C.Harrold
Grays Thurrock
1994

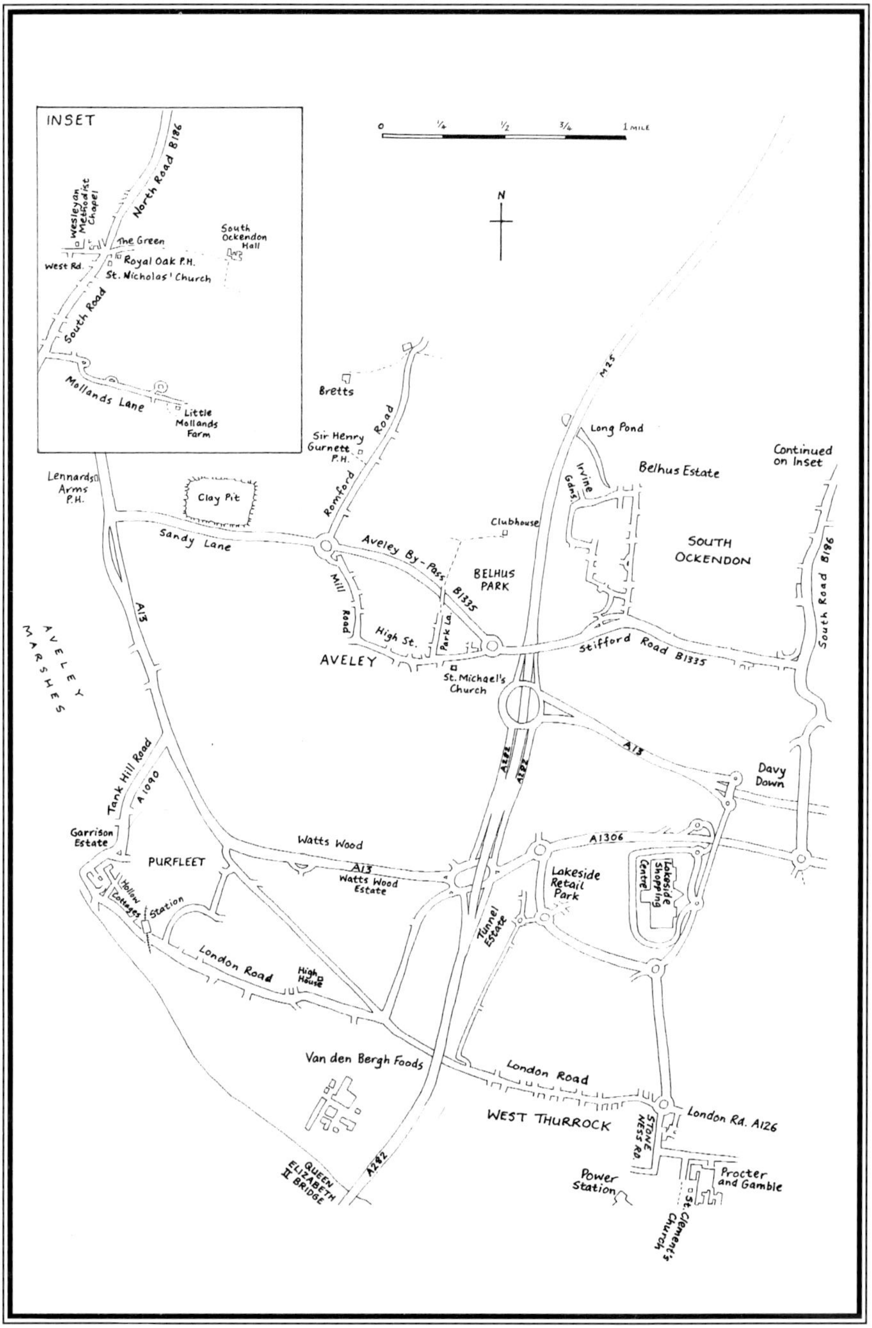
INSET
North Road B186
Wesleyan Methodist Chapel
The Green
South Ockendon Hall
West Rd.
Royal Oak P.H.
St. Nicholas' Church
South Road
Mollands Lane
Little Mollands Farm
0
1/4
1/2
3/4
1 MILE
N
Bretts
Sir Henry Gurnett P.H.
Romford Road
M25
Long Pond
Continued on Inset
Belhus Estate
Irvine Gdns.
Lennards Arms P.H.
Clay Pit
Clubhouse
SOUTH OCKENDON
Sandy Lane
Aveley By-Pass B1335
BELHUS PARK
South Road B186
Mill Road
High St.
Park La.
Stifford Road B1335
AVELEY
St. Michael's Church
A13
AVELEY MARSHES
A282
A13
Davy Down
Tank Hill Road
A1090
Garrison Estate
PURFLEET
Watts Wood
A1306
A13
Watts Wood Estate
Lakeside Retail Park
Lakeside Shopping Centre
Hollow Cottages
Station
Tunnel Estate
London Road
High House
Van den Bergh Foods
London Road
WEST THURROCK
London Rd. A126
STONE NESS Rd.
QUEEN ELIZABETH II BRIDGE
A282
Power Station
Procter and Gamble
St. Clement's Church

Western Approaches

The approach to Thurrock from the Western (London) side is marked by The Lennards public house - after the family who used to live at Belhus mansion in Belhus Park. Beyond and towards the river lie Aveley marshes. Aveley has only 1500 metres of river frontage but the marshes which adjoin those of Rainham are an interesting remnant of the past where sheep graze as they did at the time of Domesday. The Purfleet Rifle Range which occupies a significant part of the area was opened before 1910; it closed in 1994.

Turning left into Sandy Lane the road passes the "moonscape" of old clay and gravel workings which are being back-filled with London's rubbish. This led to the establishment of Aveley Methane which extracts gas evolving from the decomposition of the rubbish and treats it so that it can be burnt economically. The first use was in the boilers at the Purfleet paper mills. Electricity was generated from the steam produced by passing it through a turbine. Electricity for the national grid is produced on site at Aveley Methane by combustion of the methane and connection to a gas turbine and generator.

In this area were found the "Aveley Elephants" - a straight-tusked elephant and a mammoth. Their fossilised bones were discovered in 1964, about 100,000 years after the animals roamed the area. They are now in the Natural History Museum, South Kensington. In Thurrock's own museum at Grays are a number of Bronze Age axes which were also discovered at Aveley.

Immediately opposite the roundabout where the Aveley bypass begins is Mill House. An interesting thing about this cottage is that it is set below ground level so as to give wind clearance for the sails of the post-mill which was demolished in 1930.

Down Romford Road to the north of the roundabout is the Sir Henry Gurnett public house. This was originally called Kenningtons, a two storeycd timber-framed house with an old tiled roof, possibly 15th century in date. There are the remains of a moat and an old barn in a state of collapse. It appears to have been acquired by Henry Gurnett who died in 1345. Bretts farmhouse, taking its name from the Brett family, is a little further along the road, lying well back on the same side. This is another two-storey building using local materials of timber and brick, now covered with roughcast. It was built in the 14th century as a hall house. Like Kenningtons it has the remains of a moat which can be distinguished clearly. To the east of Romford Road is a modern estate whose streets are named after rivers.

Aveley village is reached via Mill Road. The name of the village is variously spelt in the Domesday Book of 1086 as Alvithelea, Alvileia and Alvilea. The name probably derives from "leah" the Saxon word for a meadow, belonging to Aelfgyth, who it is believed was a woman whose name means "a gift of the fairies". Aveley lies on a Roman road called Bredle Street which ran northwards from the Thames. The High Street has several old buildings but two modern ones are mentioned for different reasons. One is the hall which is the headquarters of the championship Aveley Band which was founded as the Aveley Fife and Drum Band in a back room of the Crown and Anchor in 1894. The other, dating from 1986, New Maltings, takes its name from the maltings where barley was roasted; Maltings Cottages, demolished in the 1960s, probably housed the malting workers. During the clearing of the area a copper token of Thomas Prime, an Aveley tradesman, was found. It was dated 1659. On the other side of the road is the Crown and Anchor. This has an 18th century front with a parapet, but the back is older. Nos. 54 & 56, on the same side as the church, are part of a 16th century timber-framed house whose upper floor projects along the front.

Set back from the High Street is St. Michael's church. On the right as you enter the churchyard is the memorial to members of the Barrett Lennard family of Belhus. The church is built of flint and ragstone with some Roman and 16th century brick; the tower is built of limestone. The oldest part of the church is in the early 12th century nave. Most of the windows were replaced in the 15th century when the north porch was added and the north aisle was extended alongside the tower. The clerestory and nave were built in the 16th century. The font is Norman, made of Purbeck mar-

Barrett Lennard Memorial

ble. The oak chancel screen is 15th century; the pulpit with its hexagonal sounding board is Jacobean and dated 1621. There is a carved chair of the same period in the chancel. On a beam above the pulpit are two medieval paintings; under the pulpit is a 14th century grave cover. The Barretts of Belhus and the Barrett Lennards are commemorated by a number of monuments from the 16th to the 20th century. On the floor are some fine brasses: one of Flemish workmanship lies on the south side of the chancel. The inscription in Latin reads "Here lies Ralph de Knevynton, who died the Thursday before the feast of St. Nicholas the Bishop, in the year 1370 when the Dominical letter was F". Dominical letters are the first seven letters of the alphabet used to mark the days of the week where

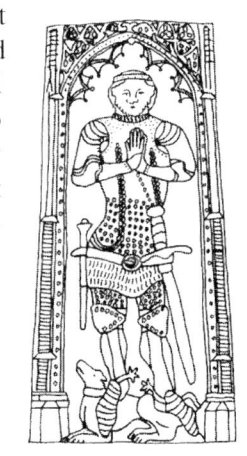

Ralph de Knevynton

"A" marks the the day of the week on which January 1 falls in any year. They are very rare on brasses. The sign of the Knight of Aveley public house in the Belhus estate is a representation of this brass. On the south wall of Aveley churchyard is a stone plaque which reads, "1830 The Ground 18 inches North of this Stone is the freehold property of the Governors of St. Thomas's Hospital"

Park Lane branches off northwards from the High Street. On the right-hand side is Courts farmhouse. This is a medieval timber-framed house with an old tiled roof. The upper storey projects, supported by three carved brackets. Park Lane originally led into Belhus Park but the route now is continued only by a footbridge which crosses the bypass into Belhus Park. Now maintained by the Local Authority, Belhus Park has a golf course and other leisure facilities. Beyond the club house the remains of Belhus mansion can just be made out in the turf. This was the family home of the Bellhouse family in the middle ages and of the Barretts from the 14th century. It was rebuilt by John Barrett c.1520 and altered in the 17th century by Edward Barrett, Lord Newburgh, who established the deer park. Dying childless in 1644 he left the estate to his "cousin" Richard Lennard on condition the latter changed his name to Barrett. Thomas Barrett, Lord Dacre inhcrited in 1738. In the 1740s and '50s he landscaped the park employing Britain's best known landscape gardener, Capability Brown. A pair of mounds and the Long Pond still survive from this period. The Long Pond was cut in half by the construction of the M25 London orbital motorway in 1980. Part of the estate is on the other side of the motorway where, with difficulty, the ice house can be found, as can more easily the remains of the kitchen garden wall in Irvine Gardens. In the park itself is an ornamental chimney which may once have connected with the sewers; it has been suggested that it was in fact the draught chimney for the steam engine which Sir Thomas Barrett Lennard installed to pump sewage out on to adjacent fields.

The house and estate were sold in 1922; some artefacts are to be seen in Thurrock Museum where there are drawings by F.S.Eden of the stained and painted glass. Much of this important armorial glass consisting of 15th century panels from Herstmonceux (Sussex) and 16th century shields commemorating the alliances of the Barrett family, is in the Philadelphia Museum and elsewhere in the U.S.A. A catalogue of this glass is in the Thurrock Museum archives. Thurrock Museum acquired more of the armorial glass in 1993. Valence House Museum at Dagenham also has some of the panelling.

Before leaving the Aveley area mention should be made of its local novelist Alice Diehl who died in 1912. She was born in Aveley. In her autobiography "The True Story of My Life" she mentions her acquaintance with the Barrett Lennards.

To the East of the M25 lies South Ockendon. Before the advent of the Belhus estate the area was largely rural. At the time of Domesday it was called Wochaduna which may be derived from the Anglo-Saxon meaning "oak pasture hill". At that time South Ockendon not only had a mill, it was also the only place in Thurrock where a hive of bees is mentioned. In 1944 the then London County Council was authorised to purchase and develop land here for housing for Londoners who would be able to work in the industries along the Thames. The course of this development is suggested by the road names on the estate which, in groups, begin with successive letters of the alphabet A to I.

Lying in the Belhus estate, which almost engulfs it, is Little Belhus. Over the cornice of the gateway is an ornamental gable on which is a cast iron panel of the Stuart Royal Arms. This 17th century house was restored by the Greater London Council in 1966; in so doing they retained the unusual two-storey porch, the shafted chimney stacks at the rear and the bellcote on the roof. Round the garden is the Tudor brick wall in which are bee-boles (niches about a metre off the ground, less than a metre wide and half a metre high) where wickerwork bee-skips were put to encourage bees to nest.

To the east of the Belhus estate is South Road leading to the village. Mollands Lane turns off this road and leads to Benton's Farm on the right hand side. This is shown as a substantial house on the Chapman and Andre map of 1777. A late medieval hall house with cross-wings, it is weatherboarded and has the features of a Georgian restoration. The green beyond marks the beginning of that part of South Ockendon which has been devoted to those in need of help. This began in 1905 when Little Mollands was used as a farm colony for the unemployed. Then in 1932 the Borough of West Ham converted Little Mollands into a place for those who at that time were called "mental defectives". 1948 saw the beginning of South Ockendon N.H.S. Hospital with a range of new buildings which can be seen from Mollands Lane. The hospital closed in 1994.

Little Mollands itself is an attractive mid-Victorian building in yellow Grays brick. Great Mollands, despite rebuilding, still shows the outline of the 17th century weatherboarded house. Grange farm to the south is an early 18th century timber-framed and plastered house. Near it is Flint Cottage, an example of an East Anglian style in unknapped flint.

Back along South Road is Quince Tree House, timber-framed and jettied on the first floor under a tiled roof; a typical medieval house. It was rebuilt in the 16th century and restored in 1983. Streets in the estate here between South Road and the railway are named after flowers.

South Ockendon is one of Thurrock's villages which has retained its village green. At its head is the Royal Oak in which exposed oak timbers add atmosphere to the interior. Part of this building has stood for 500 years; part was rebuilt in the 17th century. Originally it was called Finch's Farm; members of the Benton family who were early colonists of North America, used to live here.

Overlooking the green is the church dedicated to St. Nicholas of Myra who was Bishop of Myra, which is now in Turkey, in the 4th century. It has one of only six round church towers in Essex. This one was built of flint in the 13th century; it used to be topped by a spire but this was destroyed by lightning in the 17th century. The doorway is late Norman. Inside is a wrought iron hourglass which was first attached to the pulpit in Stuart days. A little older is the alabaster monument of 1601 to Sir Richard Saltonstall, Lord Mayor of London and Master of the Skinners' Company in Elizabethan times. He was knighted for his efforts to raise money and arms to resist the Spanish Armada. The memorial was restored in 1970 with the help of the Skinners Company, the Corporation of the City of London and the Pilgrim Trust. The carving of the seven sons and nine daughters is noticeable for the fact that the features of all of the daughters are the same, whereas those of the sons are all different and possibly lifelike. There is an early 15th century brass to Sir Ingelram Bruyn. Several cross-like masons' marks can be made out in the chancel and the north arcade.

Lying well back behind the Royal Oak at the end of an avenue are the moat and the 18th century bridge over it which led to South Ockendon Hall. All that remains of the Hall is part of the gatehouse. In 1471 the manor fell to Elizabeth, daughter of the then owner, Sir Ingelram Bruyn. Later she married William Brandon, Henry VII's standard bearer, who was slain by Richard III on Bosworth field and posthumously knighted.

In Victorian days South Ockendon manor was occupied by the Sturgeon family who also at one time lived at Sherfield House in Grays, Coppid Hall, North Stifford, The Elms, Grays and Grays Hall. They are remembered for their purchase of a royal flock of merino sheep on the death of George III in 1820. They bred these at South Ockendon for export to Australia and New Zealand where they formed a basis of the merino flocks in the antipodes.

South Ockendon Windmill, a smock-mill built c. 1820, used to be a feature of the area but it collapsed in 1977; its machinery has been re-erected in the pump house at Davy Down (q.v.). One feature which can still be seen is the large Roman barrow to the north which is surrounded by a dry ditch.

Along West Road is Street Farmhouse (16th century or earlier) which has a Georgian pedimented doorway. Just beyond is the Wesleyan Methodist chapel of 1847. North Road leads to a turning to the right before the unknapped flint wall of The Grove, formerly Groves Farm, leading to where the original Groves Manor of the Saltonstalls used to be. All that can now be seen is about thirty metres of late Tudor red brick wall, two metres high, in the middle of which is a three metre wide blocked gateway with pillars supporting a wide entablature. In the area are the remains of the manor fishponds.

The western end of Thurrock is marked by a number of areas of water, the flooded remains of former mineral workings which are now favoured by birds of interest to the naturalist and stocked with fish for local fishermen to catch. Thurrock to the north of the A13 is part of Thames Chase, a Community Forest launched in 1989 as a partnership between national statutory agencies, local government, voluntary bodies and the private sector to bring new life to the area. It includes the water sports centre of Grangewaters in one of the flooded mineral workings and also, in the ancient woodland between Aveley and the A13, the production of charcoal for local barbecues. South Ockendon is the only substantial conurbation within the Community Forest.

The road leading to the Dartford Tunnel roundabout from the west passes between Watts Wood and the Watts Wood residential estate. There is a story that these are named after Jack Watts who was a labourer in the Purfleet powder magazines in the eighteenth century. He had previously served under Governor Wall on an island off the coast of Africa where Watts witnessed the brutal flogging to death of a colleague on Wall's orders. Wall absconded on his return to England but was arrested twenty years later when Watts spoke out. As a result Wall was convicted and hanged at Tyburn. After the trial Watts resumed his duties at Purfleet but then hanged himself in the wood which afterwards took his name - but in fact the name goes back much further to 1532 and it is pure coincidence!.

To the south lie Purfleet and West Thurrock. Purfleet is approached via Tank Hill road. It might be thought that this name is associated with the Garrison Estate, several of whose street names recall the names of tanks. However it was named after the reservoir which served the garrison. The tank was on the island site which is now a nature area opposite the school.

Purfleet was designated a Conservation Area in 1985 helping to retain its character; others are at Horndon, Corringham, Orsett, the Bata Estate at East

Tilbury, Fobbing and West Tilbury. The first evidence of what is worth conserving in Purfleet is the Clock Tower, built c.1760 and restored by the local authority. It served as an entrance to the Garrison which housed the Powder Magazines. One of the five brick magazines, built in the time of George III following an explosion at Woolwich Garrrison, has been preserved, together with the proofing house. Their external appearance belies their construction which used copper nails and thickly plated copper doors and had sand in the roof space. There are no windows. They stood within an area which was walled in a series of concentric circles. Part of the inner sanctum wall may be seen in the Garrison estate. Over 50,000 barrels of gunpowder could be stored here where it was tested by firing shot from mortars. Work used to stop when a thunderstorm threatened. In 1772 Benjamin Franklin was asked to say which lightning conductor would be best; George III inquired what was Franklin's view; on being told that his political opponent was in favour of points, he declared his preference for spheres.

The Royal Hotel stands by the river. Built on the site of an earlier inn called The Ship, it was known as the Bricklayers Arms until 1845. The coming of the railway in 1854 opened up Purfleet for the day tripper from London. The Royal Hotel was known as Wingrove's Hotel (Wingrove is buried in West Thurrock churchyard) in the 1880s and 1890s and was famous for its whitebait suppers. It was frequented by the Prince of Wales who became Edward VII, and by Kitty O'Shea and Parnell. Excursion trains stopped at the station where the remains of the bridge which led into the Botany Bay Gardens, which were open to the public for about fifty years from 1859, can still be seen.

Opposite the Royal on the corner is an unpretentious house on which are the initials SW and the date 1896. Several buildings in the conservation area are part of a planned development by the one-time owners of the chalk quarries, the Whitbread family. In 1777 Samuel Whitbread M.P. purchased the manor of Purfleet as part of a larger investment in land of profits made in the brewing industry. Whitbread's house was where St. Stephen's church is now. The area beside the railway where there is now a storage depot was known as the Dipping. Here, when in 1790 chalk extraction shifted to adjacent cliffs, Whitbread built a schoolhouse and a master's house and a chapel in the following year; the remains of these buidings may still be seen. An early example of urban workers' facilities can be found in nearby Hollow

Cottages (1790 and 1800-1815) and, later, in Botany Cottages along the road. Between 1803 and 1805 the Whitbreads installed the first (horse drawn) railway in their Purfleet quarries. Above the quarries to the east of the railway on Beacon Hill, Trinity House had an experimental lighthouse from 1828 to 1870.

Bram Stoker was a visitor who described the area and especially the house Carfax, which may have been based on the former Whitbread mansion, and the mental hospital based on the Garrison House, in his novel "Dracula" which was published in 1897.

There is a ballad too which is about a celebrated murder in 1874. The chorus goes:-

> *Richard Coates, the Purfleet murderer,*
> *On Easter Monday met his doom;*
> *He killed the soldier's little daughter,*
> *Now he's dead and in his tomb.*

On the higher ground to the left on the way to West Thurrock lies High House. The site was formerly that of the manor house previously known as le Vyneyard or West Hall. High House was built in the late 17th century. Nearby is a dovecote of the same period which was renovated by the Blue Circle Cement Co. in 1976. The octagonal brick building contains over 500 nesting places.

On the marshland to the right are industrial developments among which are the works of Van den Bergh Foods which first opened in 1917. The headquarters building which was built in 1924 to resemble a Dutch town hall, illustrating the firm's Dutch origins, was erected on piles; because the surrounding land has sunk it now has a flight of steps at the entrance.

Beyond is a commanding view of the Queen Elizabeth II bridge which was opened by Her Majesty in 1991. The first Dartford Tunnel was completed in 1963. Nearly a mile long, at its lowest point it is 30 metres below high water level. A second tunnel was opened in 1980.

Little remains of the cement industry which used to dominate the area. The cement industry was introduced to Thurrock by Edmund Brooks in 1871. The original works were close to the river bank by the Wharf inn at Grays. They used clay which was pumped as a slurry from Aveley and chalk from the Thurrock anticline which was quarried nearby. Now the quarries at West Thurrock are the site of major developments: on the one hand is the Tunnel Estate whose clock tower was built in 1984; nearby is the Lakeside Retail Park, which also began in 1984 and, on the other side of the "lake", the Lakeside Regional Shopping Centre with over 300 shops and department stores which opened in 1990.

The junction between London Road and Stone Ness Road leads to West Thurrock power station and Stone Ness where the pylons which can be seen from miles around carry the national grid across the Thames. The power station was built in 1956. It was distinguished by its barrel vaulted turbine hall and by its five boilers which were very unusual in being out of doors. The power station ceased production in 1993. Next to it is the factory of soap and detergent manufacturer Procter & Gamble where production began during the Battle of Britain in 1940. The original factory by Horton and Burn was singled out by Pevsner as an example of modern functional architecture.

Dwarfed by this factory on the one side and the power station on the other lies the pilgrim church of St. Clement's. This, one of the oldest churches in Thurrock, became redundant in 1977 but was restored by Procter & Gamble to commemorate their 150th anniversary in 1987, and returned to community use in 1990. The churchyard is now a wildlife sanctuary in which are a number of rare plants: this is marked by a plaque from the Essex Churchyards Conservation Group. The present 15th century tower, with its alternate bands of flint and Reigate stone replaced an earlier circular one which was the nave of the 12th century church. Only a handful of circular-naved churches remain in this country.

The church has been refurbished with significant items from other redundant churches, such as All Saints in Grays. There are ancient bells from Pitsea, St. Michael's and Mucking and a particularly fine organ by the English maker Hugh Russell which dates from the beginning of the 19th century when it was installed in St. Runwald's, Colchester. The connection between West Thurrock and Hastings is marked by the coat of arms of that

Borough. The Manor of West Thurrock was granted to Count Robert d'Eu by William the Conqueror. The Count also built Hastings Castle and founded a collegiate church there which provided St. Clement's with its Rectors until the Reformation. A number of these men achieved considerable preferment; five attained the rank of Bishop and one, Sir Thomas Bourchier, became Archbishop of Canterbury. One of the many stories about St. Clement's is that the body of a sea captain, Nathaniel Grantham, who lived at High House in the 18th century, was discovered in 1906 by the then Rector, the Rev. Hayes, preserved in its coffin pickled in rum. Nathaniel Grantham was one of the original trustees of Palmer's school.

In Gibbs' chalk pit near Mill Lane scenes were shot for the film "The Guns of Loos" in 1927.

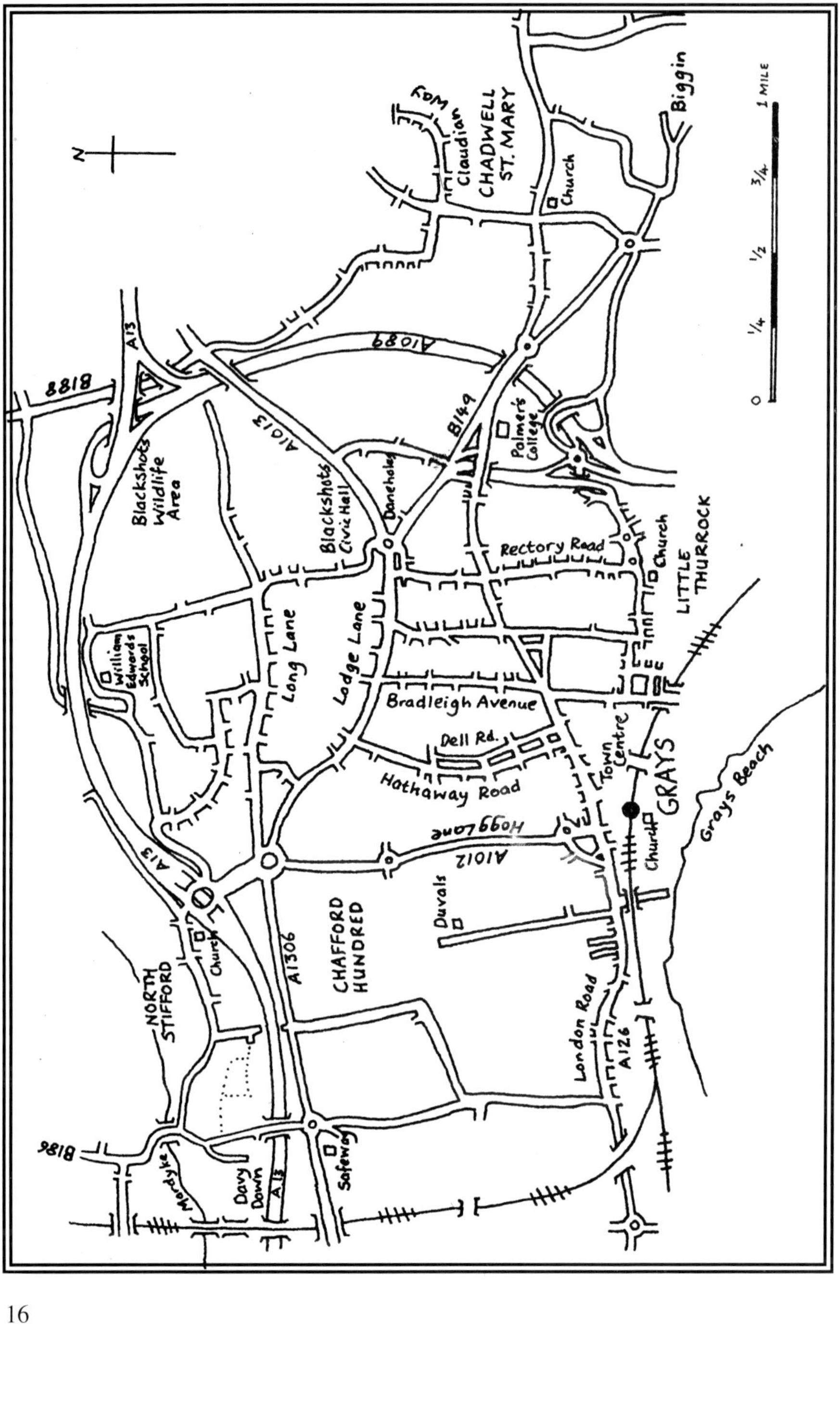
N
Claudian Way
CHADWELL ST. MARY
Biggin
Church
0
1/4
1/2
3/4
1 MILE
A13
B188
A1089
A1013
B149
Palmer's College
Blackshots Wildlife Area
Blackshots Civic Hall
Daneholes
Rectory Road
Church
LITTLE THURROCK
William Edwards School
Long Lane
Lodge Lane
Bradleigh Avenue
Dell Rd.
Hathaway Road
Town Centre
GRAYS
Grays Beach
Hogg Lane
A1012
Church
A13
Church
Duvals
CHAFFORD HUNDRED
A1306
NORTH STIFFORD
London Road
A126
B186
Mardyke
Davy Down
A13
Safeway

Central Thurrock

The exploration of central Thurrock begins at the Safeway store (1993), turning north off the main road into Pilgrims Lane. This is a 19th century romantic name but pilgrims must have passed this way to the river crossing near St. Clement's church. Passing over the A13, the countryside on the left is known as Davy Down; this is the southern gateway to Thames Chase, the community forest which was mentioned in the previous chapter. Back Lane leads to the pumping station (1921); inside are the the pumps made by the Swiss firm of Sulzer which used to raise water from the five metre diameter, fifty metre deep borehole. The machinery of South Ockendon Windmill has been re-erected in the pump house. There is a fine view of the thirteen-arched railway viaduct built by the London, Tilbury & Southend Company in 1892. In Pilgrims Lane is a small 17th century thatched cottage, one storey high with a timber framework, which was once the Harrow inn.

Stifford bridge across the Mardyke is the site of one of the earliest bridges in Thurrock; it was last rebuilt in 1925. Here is a start-point for the Mardyke Way which goes from near Aveley to Bulphan. On the high ground beyond lies Ford Place. This once impressive building was the home of James Silverlock in the 17th century and was altered in the 18th century. It was badly damaged by fire in 1987, but is being reconstructed in part. Returning up the hill to the south east, at the top is the Dog and Partridge inn. This was rebuilt on its present site back from the road in 1934 but has existed since the early 18th century when it was built on the site of the Clockhouse of 1622 of the Sheriff of Essex, Sir Thomas Gourney. Opposite is Clockhouse Lane leading to Ardale Community Home which began in 1902 as the Stepney Children's Homes. In 1935 it was an approved school and in 1969 a Community Home (Education) under the auspices of the London Borough of Newham, it closed in 1994. John Ardalle was Lord of the Manor of Stifford in the 16th century.

Opposite the recreation ground is a trio of cottages which may once have been four, called Old Post Cottage, Middlecot and Laburnum. The latter are possibly 16th century and the first one two hundred years later. Further along the High Road is another pair of timber-framed thatched cottages, two storeys high with doors in the side walls, and then another trio, Wren, Viola and Honeysuckle which were once the Oaks Inn and have weatherboarded plinths. On the other side of the road at this point stands another pair of thatched cottages which, taken with all the others, must make this one of the most attractive streets in Thurrock. Fircot and Ca-Ira are only one storey high with two dormer windows under the curve of the thatch. Nearby is The Old School House and, next to a memorial tree planted in 1959, a picturesque cottage which lies in a hollow. The 18th century cottages opposite the church are in a different style. Only one storey high, they have two attic windows and are part plaster, part weatherboarded over a timber frame.

St. Mary's church is entered by a Norman doorway enclosing a late 13th century door. The pulpit is dated 1611; attached to it is a contemporary wrought-iron hourglass stand. The church possesses an ancient parish chest which has three locks - one each for the rector and churchwardens.

Hourglass stand

There are some interesting brasses, particularly one of Radulph Perchehay, Rector 1366 to 1377, who has a fylfot (swastika) portrayed on his collar, and those to the Lathum family and to John Ardalle and his wife, all dressed in costumes of the time in which they lived. Under the carpet in the nave is an unusual brass known as a shroud brass: it is that of a shrouded priest c.1500. In his hands he is holding a heart on which is inscribed MCY (Mercy). The king post of the roof is also from the 15th century. There are the remains of a wall painting and decoration on the south side of the nave. In the chancel is a late 17th century armchair.

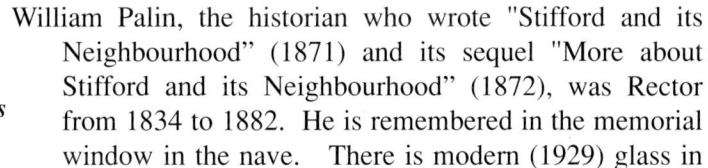

Shroud Brass c.1500

William Palin, the historian who wrote "Stifford and its Neighbourhood" (1871) and its sequel "More about Stifford and its Neighbourhood" (1872), was Rector from 1834 to 1882. He is remembered in the memorial window in the nave. There is modern (1929) glass in the south west window. Several of the wall monuments are for members of prominent local families such as Button, Freeman, Silverlock and Brooks. Herbert Brooks' father Edmund has been mentioned in connection with the cement industry. Herbert Brooks, like Palin, was a local historian. He wrote "William Palmer and his School" (1928) which is a mine of information about local people. He was living at Stifford Lodge (now the Stifford Moat House Hotel) when he died in 1931. Born into a prominent Quaker family, it was only late in life that he took a role in the Established Church.

To the east of the church is Coppid Hall, built in 1753. In the brickwork of the parapet is a tablet which reads, "This house has been antiently called Coppid Hall". Behind it is a two-storey weatherboarded and tarred granary, now a private house. Stifford Moat House Hotel still shows the outlines of a house which in its present form dates from the 18th century. Around the south front is a verandah at ground level. In the library are some pieces of 16th century glass depicting the Royal Arms.

The A13 trunk road (now the A1306) effectively divided North and South Stifford when construction began in 1923; this is even more apparent now that there is a new A13 which was opened in 1981 to bypass the bypass! North of the A13 stands Stifford Clays farmhouse; it was built about 1840 in local brick. It used to be called Flete Hall (the Mardyke was once known as the Flete river) and was possessed at one time by Sir John Clays who gave his name to the area. Building began on the Stifford Clays estate in 1952. It has street names which recall the past: Chafford was the name of the old Hundred (an ancient administrative sub-division of the Shire), Lords of the Manor included Henry de Crammavill and John Hogarth. The Manor of Flethall (hence Fleethall Grove) was also held by John Durninge and Kenwrick Grantham. John Kingsman was High Sheriff of Essex in the reign of George II. He lived at Stifford Lodge and was a trustee of Palmer's school. Palin and Simmons were rectors. The Whitmores were Lords of the Manor of Orsett. William Edwards school (1962) was named after W.H.Edwards, a master at Palmer's from 1906 to 1945, Chairman of the Governors of the school and Chairman of South Essex Divisional Executive for Education.

To the south of Stifford Clays are the Avenues which, in contrast, show piecemeal development over a number of years. Nutberry was named after the estate known as Nutburrow in 1593 and Bradleigh was named after the builder Mr Bradley of South Stifford who purchased lot no.1 in the sale of the Grays Hall Farm estate in 1921 and lived in the house he built as no.1 Bradleigh Avenue. In Lodge Lane (named after Lodge Farm) is the Methodist church which was opened in 1939. In Long Lane there were two isolation hospitals. The first hospital buildings near Blackshots Lane were put up in 1893 by Orsett Rural District Council; they included a sanatorium. In 1930 they came under Orsett Joint Hospital Board and in 1936 under Thurrock Urban District Council before reverting back to Orsett Hospital after the second world war. This hospital is now a geriatric and day care centre which became Thurrock Community Hospital (an NHS Trust) in 1993. The other isolation hospital was further along Long Lane where the Leisure Hall is now.

Off Blackshots Lane, the Blackshots complex, which includes the Civic Hall and the swimming pool, is built on the King George V Playing Fields whose purchase was aided by a grant from the King George V Memorial Fund. The buildings were designed by the Council's architect and opened in 1964. To the east of Blackshots Lane at its northern end is the Blackshots Wildlife Area which is managed by the Blackshots Residents Action Group who are affiliated to the British Trust for Conservation Volunteers.

Returning now to South Stifford, along London Road from West Thurrock there is a cast-iron boundary post about a metre high on the north side where London Road, Stifford becomes London Road, Grays. It marks the boundary between the two parishes. Further along are Castle Road and Belmont Road on the left hand side. These street names recall that Belmont Castle once stood to the north where the chalk has now been excavated. The castle was demolished in 1943, having stood there since it was built for Zachariah Button in about 1795. Flint Row opposite was once a row of mid 19th century flint cottages; this is recalled in the flint which has been incorporated in their modern counterparts. Meeson's Lane is named after the entrepreneur who came from Plaistow and developed quarries in the area. He lived at Duvals near the top of the lane set back on the right. This is a farmhouse, part of which, Randal Bingley has suggested, is the 17th century manor house which was rebuilt and enlarged in the 19th century. The north porch from Grays parish church was erected in its garden in 1867. From the very top of Meeson's Lane there is a fine panoramic view of the district.

The road almost opposite Meeson's Lane leads to another new housing estate and to the Wharf inn. This hostelry has its origin in the 18th century: it was known as The Jolly Sailor in 1769. Sometime after 1786 its name changed to The Sailor's Return - a name which lasted until the 1890s. Its present name is taken from the jetties which were built there for loading chalk.

Nearer Grays a housing estate, Badgers Dene, has been built on the floor of a quarry, but the area to the north has been retained as a nature reserve managed by the Essex Wildlife Trust. Hogg Lane leads to the Chafford Hundred development of some 5000 houses, also partly built in former chalk quarries.

Grays takes it name from Henry de Grai who was granted the manor by Richard (Coeur-de-Lion) in 1195. Grays Town Centre was redeveloped in 1970, when the Old High Street, which ran down towards the river, was demolished; improvements were made in enclosing the 1970s precinct and refurbishing the High Street in 1992. At the southern end a sculpture in mild and stainless steel was erected in 1993; it is by Ray Smith and represents a Thames barge. On it is a quotation from T.S.Eliot's poem "The Wasteland". There are also pavement plaques which recall trades and buildings once an everyday part of the High Street scene.

Thames Barge by Ray Smith

Grays town is entered from the bottom of Hogg Lane on the corner of which is the 1920s telephone exchange, now a block of flats. Beside the War Memorial of 1921, designed by A.Cox, are the magistrates courts which were built in 1929 as the police station, to the design of local architect Christopher Shiner. The Ritz cinema in Quarry Hill, now a bingo hall, opened its doors in 1940. The police station opposite was put up in 1980. Beyond the junction of the High Street and Orsett Road is the Queensgate Centre of 1988 whose name recalls The Queen's Hotel which stood alongside. This development also encompasses a block of flats and was once the

Cooperative Society department store of 1959. Grays Co-Op. was founded in 1866 by workers from the chalk quarries. Their first shop, in 1867, was in the Dutch House in the Old High Street beyond the railway crossing. Their head office building of the 1880s in Station Approach was demolished in 1994. The clock from this building was installed in Grays parish church in 1988.

In George Street is the State cinema, a Grade II listed building of 1938. When built it seated over 2000; the cinema organ is still used for recitals. In the High Street itself there is still one building of interest: this is no.53, now the Midland Bank. It has been a bank since the 1920s but in 1899 it was the Queen Victoria Temperance Hotel and a plaque of the Queen can be seen high up on the front.

Plaque of Queen Victoria

Two municipal buildings now dominate the skyline. One is the library, museum and theatre complex. Built in 1972 as a single unit, it replaced the Carnegie Free Library which was designed by Christopher Shiner in 1903. The pillared porch from this library can still be seen in the grounds of the Old Plough House motel at Bulphan. In about 1974 there began a change, first to a library agency for Essex County Council run by the Thurrock Borough Council and eventually to a local library under the direct control of Essex County Council who subsequently remodelled the interior of Grays library in 1992 and considerably reduced its stock and space to make room for the Social Services Office. On the western edge of the public open space almost opposite the Library is a line of setts which are said to come from the yard of the Old Fire Station which once stood here.

All the Borough's Civic Offices were brought together in 1992 when the large block of offices on the other side of the railway was completed.

There has been a parish church at Grays on the same site since Norman times. The present church is largely a Victorian restoration which took place in 1846 and 1867. During this rebuilding the Norman doorway now in the north porch was removed to Duvals in Meeson's Lane where it remained until 1958. On the south wall of the nave is a plaque showing the names of the vicars; at the top are several diocesan coats of arms showing that this parish was in the see of London until 1845, in Rochester diocese until St. Albans was created in 1875 and in Chelmsford from its creation in 1914. On the west wall are memorial tablets of those whose graves were moved when the church was extended in 1867. One other memorial of note is to the memory of the nineteen who lost their lives in the burning of the training ship Goliath off Grays in 1875. The west and south windows were designed by Phillipa Heskett and were installed between 1973 and 1980. Hanging in the chancel are parts of an heraldic achievement comprising a helm, gauntlet and sword. They appear to be of 16th century date. On the south wall of the chancel are the remains of a brass of about 1520 showing two wives and six daughters. The daughters have seven pairs of feet between them. The floor of the south vestry is partly laid with medieval tiles found when the Grays stationmaster's house was built in 1854. The tower houses a ring of eight bells and a service bell; seven of them came from redundant churches at West Thurrock and West Tilbury.

At the southern end of the town towards the river is the Theobald Arms of 1817 named after the Theobald family, five of whom were trustees of Palmer's school; it was formerly the Hoy. The Yacht Club was formed in 1892 by officers of the Royal Navy Artillery Volunteers. The Gull lightship which lies derelict at Grays wharf is the second oldest in European waters, having been launched in 1860. Grays Beach still possesses features which remain from the time when it was a popular resort in the early years of the 20th century: it opened in 1906.

Leading back to the Derby Road bridge is Sherfield Road which recalls the name of Sherfield House. This was the principal manor house of Grays. The home of William Palmer, the founder of Palmer's School, it was demolished in 1927. Seabrooke Rise is named after the family of brewers who were established in 1799. Their brewery was in Bridge Road just south of where the road crosses the railway.

To the north of the Orsett Road, beyond the library, is the development which began as a private estate in the 1880s and, in the 20s and 30s, continued as council housing which further developed the "Stuart" theme of the estate (because of the historical street names). These include Cromwell Road, Hampden Road named after John Hampden (1549-1643), Milton Road, Fairfax Road after the commander of the Parliamentary army, Stuart

Road, Hathaway Road, Pym Place after the Parliamentary leader, Russell Road after the General, Ireton Place after the man who married Cromwell's daughter, Wallace Road after the Governor of Belfast in 1649, and Hollis Place after one of the "five members", others of whom were Pym and Hampden. These men were impeached by Charles I in Jan. 1642, charged with an attempt to weaken the king's government. Charles came to the Commons to effect their arrest in person, an incident which led to the Civil War which broke out later that year. Lenthall Avenue is named after the Speaker of the Long Parliament, Thurloe Walk (where a Bronze Age hoard was found in 1930) after the politician John Thurloe, Ludlow Place after Edmund Ludlow who escaped abroad after the Restoration, Lisle Place and Lucas Road after Sir George Lisle and Sir Charles Lucas, heroes of the seige of Colchester (1648), and Albemarle Close after George Monck, made Duke of Albemarle for his part in restoring Charles II.

Further up Orsett Road, Dell Road is on the left. This name recalls The Dell which was the home of Alfred Russell Wallace from 1872 to 1876. The date 1872 is prominent on the facade of the house. He is remembered for formulating a theory of evolution by natural selection independently and contemporaneously with Darwin. It was here that he completed "The Geographical Distribution of Animals". He was also co-founder of the British National Union of Spiritualists in 1873. The garden which Wallace made in imitation of a Welsh valley below the house - in an area described by Palin in 1850 as "a fairyland with its deep and picturesque ravine" - has been recovered by Treetops School which was built on the site of The Elms, the house next door to the Dell.

Opposite Dell Road is Grays Park. This was where Meeson had one of his brickworks. At the top of the hill is Grays Hall of 1869 which replaced the older building on the other side of Orsett Road which was demolished in 1901. Grays Hall is now a youth centre. Down Bridge Road are the Bridge Road Schools first opened in 1898. It was here in the summer of 1936 that "Lord Haw Haw" gave a lecture on the aims of the British Union of Fascists. Part is in use as Grays Centre for Adult Education. On the outside of the old building is the ledge on which pupils used to sharpen their slate pencils. At the top of the passageway beyond the schools is another cast-iron boundary post; on it are the initials GTP and LTP which refer to Grays and Little Thurrock parishes. This post has been moved from the boundary to be used to narrow the passageway here.

Another building in this area of Grays is the former All Saints church, now Thurrock Christian Fellowship. This began as a mission in John Street in 1886. In 1926 it became All Saints and the church erected in 1927 was designed by Sir Charles Nicholson. It became redundant in 1986 but some of its fitments are now in St. Clement's church, West Thurrock.

Palmer's Avenue was built in 1890 to bypass a section of the old Southend road (now Bradleigh and Cresthill Avenues) which has an awkward right-angled bend, and to provide a grand approach to the town. Many of the houses in this area of Grays, including nearly all of High View Avenue, were built by Ben Pipe who built and lived in no.4 Cresthill Avenue in the early twenties. In the entrance to the passageway between College Avenue and St. George's Avenue is another misplaced boundary stone belonging to Grays and Little Thurrock parishes.

At the junction of Southend Road and Chadwell Road is a stone from Palmer's School which used to stand there. It is dated 1934 and has on it the arms of Essex and the motto of the school "Monumentum Aere Perennius" (A Monument more lasting than Bronze). William Palmer founded his school for boys in 1706; the first building was beside the parish church, the second in Orsett Road. The one which used to be here was built in 1874; a girls' wing was added in 1876. The girls moved to a new school at Chadwell in 1931; to this were added an open air amphitheatre in 1954 and a new hall in 1964. In 1971 the foundation became a sixth form college which was finally located on the former girls' school site in 1977. The old school with its tiered science lecture theatre and indoor swimming pool was subsequently demolished. Palmer's Trustees added a new lecture theatre on the Chadwell site in 1992; further additions and alterations have been made to meet the needs of sixth form education and of a wider responsibility with the advent of grant maintained status as Palmer's College in 1993. In 1930 Roman funerary pots were found in the school grounds and in 1970 a Roman pottery kiln was excavated on the playing field in front of the school.

North of the sixth form college near Daneholes roundabout there is evidence of another local industry in the form of deneholes. These are in Hangman's

Wood, a remnant of ancient woodland: they are shafts cut down into the chalk which have several chambers leading off from the bottom, the remains of early chalk workings. The majority appear to have been dug between 1300 and 1550 - the latter date marking the ascendency of the open cast mining system over shaft mining. Half hidden at the bottom of the slope in the open space known as The Dipping, between Woodview and Rectory Road, is a discarded Essex County Council boundary post.

Part way down Rectory Road is the War Memorial at Turp's Corner. George Turp became the tenant of Mallins Farm, which stood on the north side of the junction, in the early 1890s. Before that this used to be called Polly Cook's Corner. Polly was the daughter of a previous owner of Mallins; she set up a dame school here in the 1830s.

South of Turp's Corner, the Globe Works were established in the old brick-workings after the first world war. Brickearth deposits were found here in the 18th century, bricks from this area being used in the construction of the martello towers. The family of Ingram were brickmakers who in 1822 followed the achievement of the Whitbreads at Purfleet and established a tramway for the transport of bricks to the quayside. When demolitions were taking place in in the Globe Works in 1961 flint tools of Clactonian (old stone age) hunters were found - the earliest evidence of human occupation in the Thames valley.

St. Mary's church at the southern end of Rectory Road is in Early English style, restored in 1878-90. In the south wall is a tall blocked Norman doorway, on the outside of which is a scratch dial. This is a form of sundial, sometimes called a mass dial, where grooves were used to mark the times of church services before mechanical clocks came to be commonly used in the 15th century (see illustration in chapter on "The Fenland"). A metal rod known as a gnomon was inserted in the hole to cast a shadow on the grooves. In the nave is a plain oak pulpit which bears the inscription R 1700 C and in the chancel are a 14th century sedilia and piscina. The school next door to the church was built in 1871: it has a clocktower surmounted by a weathervane which recalls the origins of the building now that it has become a private house.

Almost opposite the church in a lane past the post office, at the end of the wall close to the ground, is the remnant of another cast-iron post which marked the boundary between Little Thurrock and Grays parishes. Across the junction is Tyrrell's Hall Club. This is on the site of Tyrrell's Hall which was demolished in 1782.

Along Dock Road towards Tilbury is the Bull inn. This was originally a farmhouse dating from the 17th century; it was licensed to serve ale in 1770. The road to Tilbury and Chadwell passes an estate on the right whose roads are named after wild flowers. Beyond the road to Tilbury Chadwell Place can be seen above Marshfoot Road. It was approached from the marshes by a clearly defined manorway which has eroded six metres down through the gravel bank. Chadwell Place was once called Long House Manor. It is basically an early 18th century house though parts of the back may be older.

The Chadwell bypass leads back to the skyline tower block of Thurrock College which was built between 1954 and 1960 to the design of the County Architect H.C.Connolly. The College achieved grant maintained status in 1993, having started life as Thurrock Technical College.

Chadwell St. Mary owes its prominence to the gravel beds on which it was built. A hoard of silver Roman coins, one with the head of Sabina on it, was found near Sandy Lane. Chadwell appears in Domesday as Celdewella which means a cold spring. Also in Domesday is the name of Aluric who, like Sabina, has given his name to a Chadwell street. Other historical names are Claudian Way from the Roman Emperor Claudius, Defoe, Morant the Essex historian, and the writers Kingsley, Ruskin and Meredith. One name yet to be used is that of Chadwell author Charles Whitton who wrote two novels in the 1920s.

The church is dedicated to St. Mary. The basic plan of the nave is Norman and both north and south doorways remain. The one nearest the road has a decorated tympanum above the door. An Early English chancel has been added to the nave and the tower was added a century later. There are rood stairs in the south east corner of the nave and several scratch dials. One is outside half way up the quoined south east corner of the nave. Two more are inside the vestry door on what used to be the outside of the south doorway. There are votive crosses on the jamb of this doorway. In the graveyard, to the east, is an interesting grave to a Japanese seaman, Kadzuo

Yamazaki, aged 22, who in 1899 died in the execution of his duty in a fire on board the Nippon Yusen Kaisha.

At the top of the hill, across the road from the church, is Sleeper's farm. This is a late 15th century timber-framed house under a thatched roof. The cross-wing at the southern end is jettied back and front and is supported on brackets. Inside, remains of the original timbers can still be seen. During reconstruction work in 1967 a bundle of parish officers' papers was found which had remained hidden for 130 years.

At the foot of the hill Biggin Lane on the left leads to the small community of Biggin.

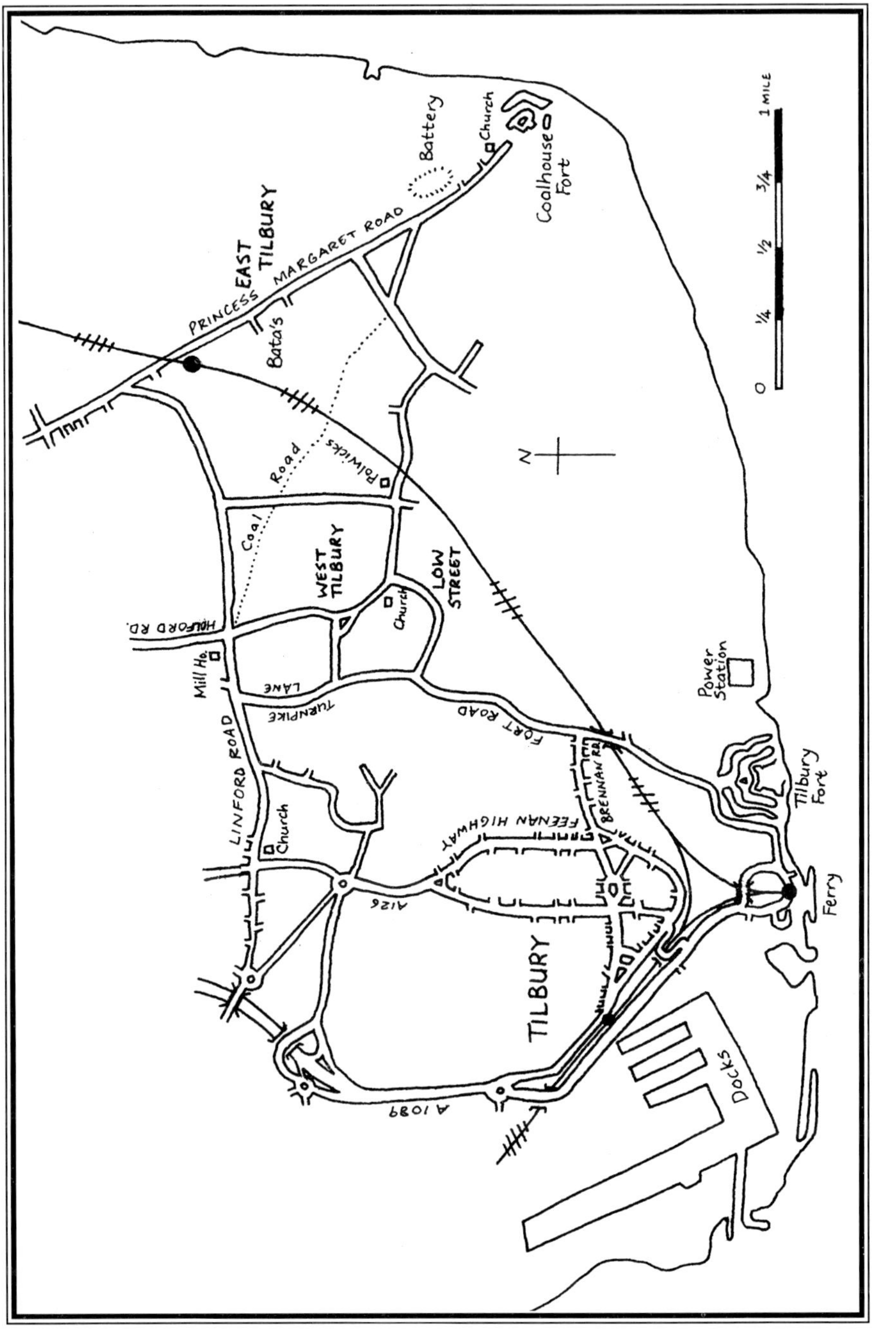
EAST TILBURY
PRINCESS MARGARET ROAD
Battery
Church
Coalhouse Fort
Bata's
Polwicks
Coal Road
WEST TILBURY
LOW STREET
Church
HOLFORD RD.
Mill Ho.
TURNPIKE LANE
FORT ROAD
LINFORD ROAD
Church
FEENAN HIGHWAY
BRENNAN RD.
A126
TILBURY
A1089
Docks
Power Station
Tilbury Fort
Ferry
N
0
1/4
1/2
3/4
1 MILE

The Tilburys

Beyond Biggin Lane across the marshes lies the town of Tilbury which owes its existence to the establishment of Tilbury Docks in 1886. Initially tenements were provided for the labourers in The Dwellings, the last of which survived until the 1960s, and for the staff, two rows of houses whose name Tilbury Gardens is still on the map to the west of the railway station although the Gardens themselves were demolished in 1993. The first speculative housing enjoys street names which are reminiscent of Tilbury's earliest world-wide connections - Sydney, Calcutta, Toronto, Wellington and Bermuda. After the end of the Great War many local councils were eager to embark on housing schemes to provide homes for their people. Tilbury Urban District Council was given permission to build 1520 "cottages" and Mr Brennan (of Brennan Road), Chairman of the UDC, cut the first sod in 1920. In 1924 the estate began using a building system based on triangular blocks. The hollow blocks were made at Tilbury with cement and industrial waste materials. Electricity was switched on to the estate in 1927 by Mr Feenan (of Feenan Highway), the then Chairman of the UDC.

The Victorian iron bridge of 1896 crosses the railway which first came to Tilbury in 1854. Beyond are the extensions to the docks which were carried out between 1963 and 1978 to make Tilbury a major container port. The cottage hospital in Ferry Road (1925) has long gone but at the end of the road is what is now styled the London International Cruise Terminal. This building is part of the 1930s development of the floating landing stage which was opened by Prime Minister Ramsay Macdonald. In his speech he said, "I hope that many happy people will leave it on prosperous voyages and many satisfied people will use it to get home again" - echoing the future motto of the Borough of Thurrock "Secundum Tamesim Quovis Gentium" - "By Thames to all the Peoples of the World". During the Second World War the Tilbury Hotel, a landmark commanding the entrance to Tilbury Dock was destroyed by enemy action, but Tilbury played a major part in two key enterprises. The first of these was the construction, in temporary specially constructed dry docks, of the Mulberry Harbours of floating breakwaters which were sunk in position for the invasion code-named "Operation Overlord". The other was code-named "Pluto" - the pipeline under the ocean: seventeen pipelines were constructed in the northern part of the docks and laid across the Channel to supply the armies of the Allies. In more recent times scenes from an "Indiana Jones" film were shot here.

The early years of the docks were stormy ones. Tilbury was the scene of the first successful dock strike which took place in 1889. A docker earned 4d an hour for an average weekly wage of 16/- (80p), compared to an estimated minimum subsistence wage of 25/- per week. The strike, for "the full round orb of the docker's tanner (6d)", was noteworthy for its unity of purpose, its solidarity and its organisation, which owes much to a remarkable man, Ben Tillett. He is described by the Dictionary of National Biography as "the man of the world with a spark of genius and imagination".

Another man whose name is associated with Tilbury is Daniel Defoe. In 1695 he was secretary, and subsequently owner, of a brick and pantile works. Randal Bingley has unravelled the evidence to show that Defoe's house and factory were at the triangle now formed by the junction of the railway into and out of what was Tilbury Riverside station. In 1703 Defoe was put in the pillory and imprisoned in Newgate (where the Old Bailey is now) for publishing "The shortest way with Dissenters", of which he was one. In it with heavy irony he set out an argument for using violent means to keep protestant dissenters from enjoying religious toleration.

This was meant to be a satire on the High Church party but he had made a great error of judgement. Not long after this incident his business failed and Defoe concentrated on his writing, publishing Robinson Crusoe in 1719.

To the east lies the World's End inn. This is a two-storey weatherboarded building with a slate roof, rebuilt on its present site in the late 18th century and modernised in 1983. It was long connected with the ferry to Gravesend. The ferryhouse was originally at the front of Tilbury Fort and in 1694 the Tilbury to Gravesend ferry was claimed by the Governor of the Fort. At about the same time the Corporation of Gravesend were able to obtain the rights to the Gravesend to Tilbury ferry from the manor of Parrock. In 1851 Gravesend Corporation obtained a lease of the Board of Ordnance Tilbury-Gravesend ferry and started services using a tug which transported passengers, livestock and goods in both directions. White Horse Ferries acquired the ferry service in 1991, but in 1992 this new service with a brand new ferry was challenged by the Crown Commissioners who demanded a huge fee. Subsequently this was significantly reduced so that the ferry could continue to operate.

One man who used the ferry and its inn was Samuel Pepys: he writes that on 3 Aug. 1665 he came "to the Blockehouse (Tilbury Fort), over against Gravesend, where we staid a great while, in a little drinking house.....I, by and by, by boat to Gravesend". He was in the area again on 24 Sept. (the Lord's Day), "Being about Grayes, and a very calm curious morning, we took our wherry, and to the fishermen, and bought a great deal of fine fish, and to Gravesend and had part of it dressed".

Detail of Tilbury Fort

Tilbury Fort has been described as the best preserved and in many ways the finest example of late seventeenth century military engineering in England. The present building, designed by Bernard de Gomme in 1670, in response to the Dutch incursion into the Medway in 1667, replaced a much smaller blockhouse erected in 1539 in the reign of Henry VIII. The impressive watergate is a reminder that Charles II visited the fort in 1671 at about the time it was built. There was a remodelling of the east bastion under General Gordon in 1868 and extensive restorations in the 1980s. The fort is now in the care of English Heritage. Sheridan's play "The Critic" was put on at Drury Lane in 1779; Act II scene 2 is marked "Tilbury Fort, two sentinels discovered asleep..."

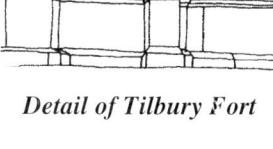

Beyond the fort is Tilbury power station. There were once two power stations here. "A" was built in 1958 but has been decommissioned; "B" first produced power in 1967. It burns up to 11200 tonnes of coal and disposes of 1400 tonnes of ash daily via the building trade. Very little dust leaves the 180 metre high chimneys. It may not be generally known that between here and Gravesend is the Thames tunnel nearest the sea. This three metre diameter shaft, approximately two kilometres in length was the first to be driven through the chalk stratum in free air, which is safer to work in than compressed air. The 55 metre deep tunnel carries twelve 400kV cables which are immersed in cooling water. There is a walkway but it is not open to the public. Within the grounds of the former "A" station is the Energy and Environment Centre run jointly by National Power, Essex Education Authority and the Essex Wildlife Trust. Opened in 1990, up to 5000 schoolchildren a year visit the centre's classroom and follow the nature trail, taking part in such activities as pond dipping. Next door is Anglian Water's deep shaft computerised sewage treatment plant.

To the north on the escarpment can be seen West Tilbury. Fort Road leads back across the marshes and up Gun Hill. The name Gun has been attributed to the landowner, Gonville and Caius College Cambridge; if so, it is likely to be prior to 1557 when Dr. Caius refounded Gonville Hall.

Across to the east at the foot of the hill a grove of poplars can be distinguished on Cooper's Shaw. These were planted during the Second World War as a wartime measure by subsidy from Bryant & May to provide (eventually) wood for making matches.

Gun Hill runs north into Turnpike Lane. At the top of Turnpike Lane to the west are Atherton Gardens; on the east side of the Gardens is the old parish boundary of West Tilbury. It is marked by a raised bank on which bluebells flourish beneath gnarled oaks, both indicative of the age of the boundary.

Linford Road to the east runs past Mill House. Next to it is the base of West Tilbury mill. There is a post mill at this point on John Walker's map of 1584 and on Chapman and Andre's map of 1777 there is a smock mill. Morant referred in 1768 to a windmill standing at the point where he thought a military camp had been set up at the time of the Armada. Recent research has confirmed that this field to the east of Holford Road was indeed the place where Queen Elizabeth I reviewed her troops in 1588 and where she made her famous speech which contains the stirring words, "I am come amongst you resolved, in the midst and heat of battle, to live or die amongst you all, to lay down for my God, and for my kingdom, and for my people, my honour and my blood, even in the dust. I know I have the body of a weak and feeble woman, but I have the heart and stomach of a King". Queen Elizabeth would have travelled along Holford Road on her way to Saffron Gardens. Another rider along this ancient road was highwayman John

Nevison who, after crossing the Thames from Kent at Tilbury Fort, is said to have ridden non-stop to York - a tradition noticed by the historian Macaulay, which represents Nevison as the real hero of the ride popularly attributed to Dick Turpin. Nevison was caught and hanged in York in 1685.

Nearby was a steam mill which was demolished in 1975. It was conveniently situated at this point where there is a junction in Blue Anchor Lane to the south with a bridleway called the Coal Road. Running from here back down to Coalhouse Fort where there was once the coal jetty, this is probably an ancient trackway which got its name in the 18th century from its use to supply coal to Grays and the surrounding area, possibly to the military as far away as Warley barracks in the 19th century. It crosses an area of former strip farming; a reminder of this, at TQ 67 674779 (opposite the Bata factory), is a hard brown stone on the southern edge of the trackway. On it are the letters E C L, the unidentified initials of a common strip owner. Seven miles of the "Coal Road" have been identified across Thurrock.

Blue Anchor Lane gets its name from the public house which still exists as a private house of that name on the east side of the road. Standing back on the opposite side of the road is Marshall's. This is a late 16th century hall house which was reconstructed in 1974. On the eastern side of the road is a cast-iron charity post inscribed with the name "Sir John Cass 1868". There is another like it in Thurrock Museum. Such posts distinguish the plots of land of tenants of Holford Farm whose rents made up part of the income of the Aldgate School founded by Sir John Cass in 1710. These particular

Charity Post

lands were added to the school endowment under his will of 1718, to be used to provide salaries for the Master and Mistresses and clothing for the children. Unfortunately Sir John died most dramatically just before the will was completed, being seized of a fatal haemorrhage in the very act of signing. The quill pen which he was using was stained red with blood, a circumstance which has given rise to the custom, still kept up by the pupils of the school, of wearing a red quill on their coats on Founder's Day, 20 February. Sir John Cass College is a continuation of the Foundation.

West Tilbury, like South Ockendon, still has its village green. The pillory is modern, but around the green are several buildings of note. Just off to the west is the old post office, now a private house, which has double bay 19th century windows. On the north east corner is White House Farm (painted white), formerly Blue House Farm (when it was painted blue), weatherboarded as it was in the 18th century. To the west are the Old Bakery c.1835, and next to it Well House. The latter is in two blocks, one of the 18th century; the other seems to be a cross wing of an earlier hall house obscured behind a brick facade. The house is associated with the large rectangular pond next door which was cut away to exploit the spring which rises here.

In the distance is St. James' church which has an early 12th century chancel and nave. Legend has it that in 1648 the church was sacked by Fairfax's soldiers who were on their way to the siege of Colchester. Following the collapse of the tower in 1712, it was rebuilt in part. Much rebuilding was done in 1879 and further restoration work was carried out in 1883. After becoming redundant in 1983 the building became a private house. Some of the church furniture was removed to the chapel at Tilbury Fort.

Next to the church is West Tilbury Hall whose adjoining weatherboarded barn was converted into a private house in 1977. The Hall itself is depicted in colour on John Walker's map of 1584 - this map is the earliest surviving example of the work of John Walker senior. At the rear was one of the mineral water wells which led to an attempt to turn West Tilbury into a Spa in the 18th century. The Rector's well was in church field, down the hill past the church on the right. The effect of the waters was first noticed by farmer John Kellaway in 1727 when it relieved his gout. A treatise about the medicinal properties was written by Dr. J. Andree in 1736 and a further account appeared in 1779. Both wells were visible in 1907 when the water was sampled and analysed. The Rector's well was contaminated but the Hall well was shown to contain much Calcium Carbonate and salt which might explain its reputedly medicinal properties.

Tilbury is of Saxon origin, "Tilla" being the name of a chieftain and "burg" meaning a fort. The Venerable Bede (673-735) in his "Ecclesiastical History of the English Nation", says that St. Cedd, having received the episcopal dignity, built churches in several places...also in that which is called Tilaburg. Gervaise de Tilbury (floreat 13th century) wrote various books which established his literary fame. The best known concerns the duties of the exchequer. He was born in the village but spent most of his life abroad.

Church Road leads to Low Street on the way to East Tilbury. Here is the 15th century house Condovers, now reverted to the name Walnut Tree Farm which it was called in 1793, following restoration in 1974. This is a timber framed house, gabled with a jettied cross wing and a weatherboarded plinth. The name relates to the fact that there were seven walnut trees planted outside by Church Road, the last of which survived until the 20th century.

Across the way is Polwicks. It has two parallel roofs hipped behind a yellow stock brick facade. Improvements were made in 1710-20 and the house was remodelled in 1830-35 when Ingrams of Little Thurrock supplied the bricks for the front. Once the home of local historian Col. Loftus it was owned at one time by Sir Matthew Fetherstonhaugh who purchased the great house of Uppark in Sussex, leaving Polwicks to his son Sir Harry. Sir Harry took Emma Hart as his mistress. Later Emma married Sir Wm. Hamilton and as Lady Hamilton became Nelson's mistress.

Station Road leads past Polwicks to the level crossing where the remains of Low Street station can be discerned. Beyond, a small industrial estate was established in 1960 in the quarry where the Low Street brickworks used to be. In 1975 a fragmentiser was installed to convert old cars into bits of metal for recycling.

Up a turning which used to go to a tip is Bucklands, another 18th century house. Here lived Col. R.H. Williams, author of "My Life with the Border Ruffians" (in the U.S.A.). Opposite is Bowaters Farm. Here was an important anti-aircraft gun site during the Second World War. The remains of the associated buildings are still there.

The road down to Coalhouse Fort passes an overgrown area on the left in which is the East Tilbury Battery which dates from 1891. It was equipped with guns with "disappearing mounts" which meant that the guns sank out of sight once they had fired. The installation was profiled into the contour of the hill and was called a "Twydell" battery after the village in Kent where the first experiments were made of this design. Coalhouse Fort itself originated as a blockhouse half a mile from the present fort, designed for artillery in 1540. This was D-shaped like the first Tilbury Fort and two storeys high. In response to French threats a new fort was built at East Tilbury in 1799, but this was abandoned after the defeat of Napoleon. Increasing concern about the French and the development of iron-clad warships led to a re-appraisal of coastal defences by a Royal Commission in 1859. This led to the construction of Coalhouse Fort, the later stages of which from 1865 were supervised by General Gordon; it was completed in 1874. During the Second World War two unique 5.5" guns from the battleship H.M.S.Hood were mounted in camouflaged shelters on the roof and the Fort became a centre for checking the efficacy of magnetic mine defences on ships in the Thames. In 1962 the Fort was acquired by Thurrock Urban District Council for development as a riverside amenity. In 1983 conservation and restoration of the structure commenced by the Coalhouse Fort Project manned by enthusiastic volunteers, aided in 1984 by the Manpower Services community programme. This long-term effort has led to the Fort being open to the public on one day a month when there are guided tours of the defence system, and to the holding of nostalgic, yet authentic, military events.

In the Thurrock Museum is one of the stones which once marked the boundary of the Whitechapel Charity School land. This charity was established by the Rev. Ralph Davenant, vicar of a London parish in 1680, who gave goods and plate to build a school in Whitechapel. An unknown lady gave a further £1000 in 1701 which enabled the trustees to purchase the estate at East Tilbury known as Castle Farm. Part was leased to the Govt. in Napoleonic times for the erection of a battery where the East Tilbury battery is now. The Davenant Foundation School is now in Loughton.

St. Katherine's church was formerly dedicated to St. Margaret when the north arcade was built with its carved capitals. The south wall has 14th century windows inserted into the remains of a south arcade. The south aisle may have fallen when the tower fell in the 17th century. There is no evidence to back the story that the tower was destroyed by the Dutch during their raid up the Medway in 1667, although cannon balls have been found at Fobbing and near Coalhouse Fort. There is a 16th century font and an Elizabethan pulpit. There are two Royal Arms on the north wall. Both are of the time of George III: one of them is the West Tilbury board, fetched to East Tilbury in 1982. They depict the arms of England & Wales, Scotland and Ireland and the arms of Hanover. The latter were imported into our heraldry when George Lewis, Elector of Hanover, became King on the death of Queen Anne in 1714, in order to preserve the Protestant Succession. The Royal Arms here are representations of the second Hanoverian period when the Hanoverian arms were placed on an escutcheon in the centre ensigned with an Electoral Bonnet. The Holy Roman Empire was dissolved in 1806 but the arms of its office of Arch-Treasurer remained on the Hanoverian arms. In 1801 the royal Arms had changed by the removal of the fleurs-de-lis of France, the french kingdom claimed by England since 1340 having been abolished by revolution. A third Royal Arms is high above the crossing; now indecipherable, these are possibly 16th century when such arms were first introduced to churches. In front of the vicar's stall is a mosaic set in the floor of a fish, designed and executed by pupils of East Tilbury School in 1966. Some coffin plates are preserved in the church; they were found in a vault early in the 20th century. At the west end overhead is a Catherine wheel presented in 1960 by the Rev. Whitwham in memory of his parents. It was made in Orsett and decorated by the Orsett blacksmiths Mortimer & Smith. In the church is the single bell dated 1629. It is inscribed "Soli Deo Gloria" and is by William Oldfield of York.

During the Great War soldiers of the Royal Artillery and Royal Engineers thought to use the stone lying near the church to rebuild the tower as the Gordon Memorial tower and to provide a war memorial. The vicar gained permission direct from the War Office and in due course a new tower began to arise. The memorial took the form of an obelisk surmounted by the emblem of the Royal Engineers. The monument when unveiled was seven metres high. However the garrison had a magazine in which their patriotic efforts were described and they sent a complimentary copy to their commanding officer who had neither heard of nor sanctioned the scheme. A high level visit followed in which the troops were ordered to pull down the monument, which was on W.D. property. The tower was left unfinished as the General had no authority on church land. There is a memorial stone in the wall of the tower which although dated 1917 commemorates the war of 1914-18.

Across the road from the church is the vicarage of 1834. In the porch is part of a fire insurance sign.

To the east, past the East Tilbury battery, is an area in which are Red Hill sites. Dating from Roman times, they are places where salt production was carried out by evaporation of salt water.

Princess Margaret Road leads north to an estate where there are more roads with royal names. This is the Bata estate, built for the workers of the shoe factory opposite in 1933. The founder of the Company, Thomas Bata from Zlin in the former Czechoslovakia, was killed in a plane crash in 1932; he is commemorated outside the factory by the only public statue in Thurrock. It was erected in 1955 and temporarily removed to Zlin for the celebration of the parent Company's centenary in 1994. The interesting communal enterprise comprised 300 homes, four dormitory buildings, a swimming pool, tennis courts, cinema (now the village hall), a model farm, an hotel (now a block of flats), shops, a memorial garden, an orchard, a fire station, a school and a sports ground. This masterplan was devised by architects in Czechoslovakia who had worked with Le Corbusier and Frank Lloyd Wright. The resultant factory buildings and estate housing, characterised by its uniform layout and flat roofs, are based upon those of Zlin. This Eastern European influence represents a rare local example of "modern movement" building; it is now a Conservation Area.

Thomas Bata
1870 - 1932

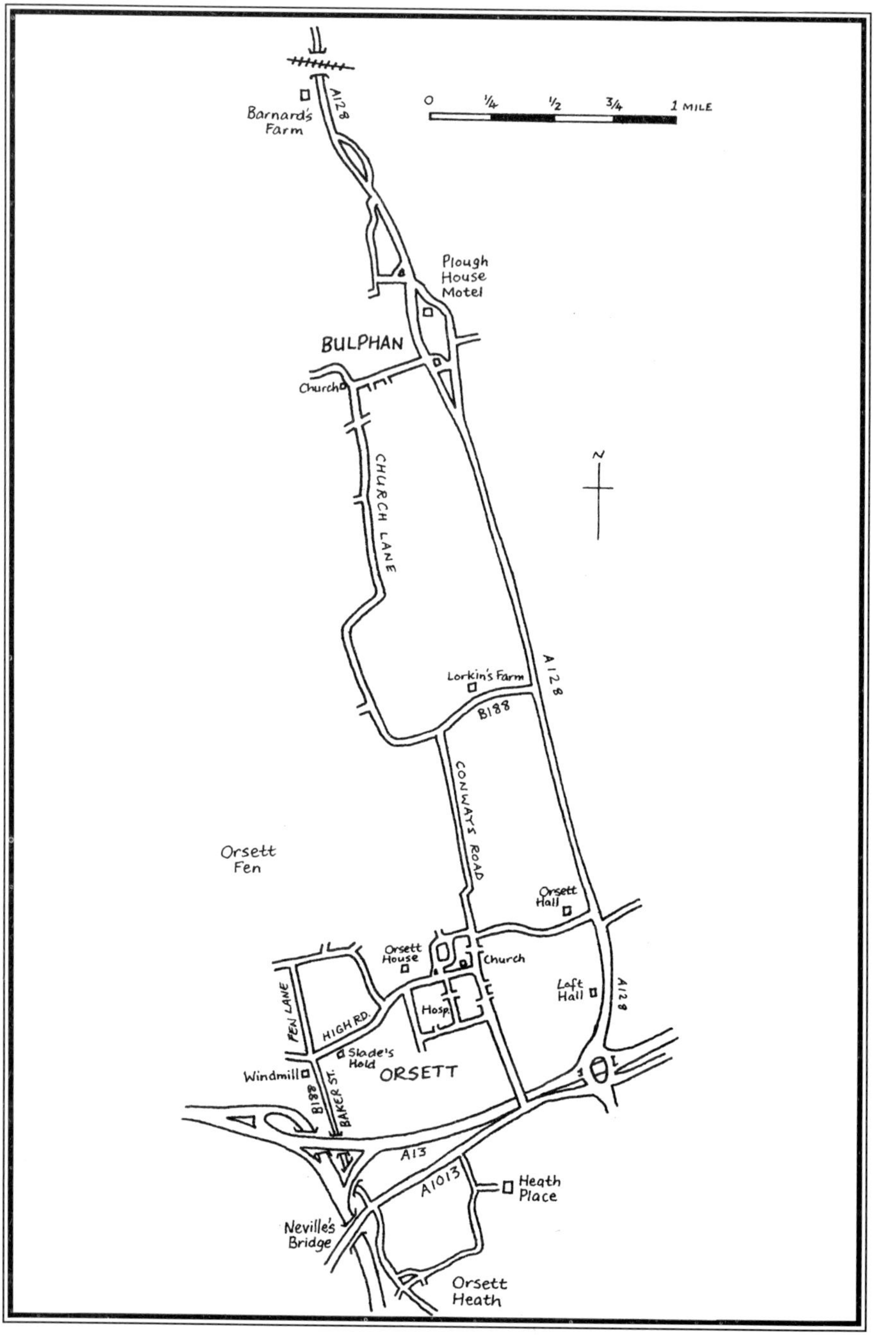
0
1/4
1/2
3/4
1 MILE
N
Barnard's Farm
A128
Plough House Motel
BULPHAN
Church
CHURCH LANE
Lorkin's Farm
B188
CONWAYS ROAD
Orsett Fen
Orsett Hall
Orsett House
Church
Laft Hall
Hosp.
FEN LANE
HIGH RD.
Slade's Hold
Windmill
ORSETT
B188
BAKER ST.
A13
A1013
Heath Place
Neville's Bridge
Orsett Heath

The Fenland

Exploration of the Fenland begins at Nevilles bridge on the A1013 over the A1089 from Tilbury. On the left is the turn to Baker Street; near the corner is a small weatherboarded thatched cottage which was built in the late 17th/early 18th century. Further along the main road on the right is Whitecrofts, attractively styled in Georgian brick with parapetted wings. It still has its farm buildings round it; on the roof of one of them is a weather-vane fretted with the date 1773.

Hornsby Lane on the right leads to Heath Place. This is a timber-framed house of the 17th century. Behind is a granary and a three-seater wooden privy; in the garden is a Victorian grotto c.1870. The first known occupant of the house was J'atte de Hathe in 1372. Martha Randall lived here in the "golden" Victorian age of the mid 19th century. She has left us her diary which covers the years 1858 (when she was sixteen) to 1861. She paints a picture of life for a young lady of her time and station as the daughter of a tenant farming family. Here are a few extracts from a transcript in the Thurrock Museum:-

Tues. 10 Aug. 1858   I went to the cricket match at East Tilbury between married and single. In the evening the boys went down to the Fort to see the fireworks let off in honour of the Queen embarking at Gravesend.
Tues. 19 Oct. 1858   Mama and I went to London. It was a pouring wet day. We went to Segatt's to see the picture of the Derby Day (a new picture by Frith).
Thurs 23 June 1859   (The picnic) Fannie and I got up rather early. We walked down to the station (at Purfleet) to meet the London people. When we went in the grounds we played ball and then went up to the Light House. After dinner we walked about and danced and played rounders. When it got too dark to do anything we walked up to the Hotel....where there was scarcely room to stand, but it was great fun.
Wed. 28 Dec. 1859   (Digby Wingfield's Coming of Age) This evening we are going to a ball at the Hall. This morning gifts are to be distrib-

uted to nearly all the poor of the parish. It is pouring with rain. I am very sorry as some of the poor have to come from a good way. We were received by Mr Baker who left for town after dancing the first dance with Mrs Newcome. Digby was not there at all. We left at 4 o'clock.

Further along Hornsby Lane towards Orsett Heath is Heath Lodge, a two-storey weatherboarded cottage with a thatched roof. It was originally built as two cottages in 1790-1800.

Back on the main road the land rises up Potash Hill past Potash Cottages which refer to the residues which contained the potash from charcoal burning nearby. On the right before the Orsett Cock roundabout is a thatched building once known as Prattocks, now Murrell's Cottage on the one side and The Thatches on the other. On the A128 towards Brentwood lies Loft Hall, in red brick of 1820-30 with a lesser extension of 1840-50. An upper window has been sealed over and painted on the outside with imitation glazing bars.

Next comes Orsett Hall. This was the seat of the Lord of the Manor until the estate was sold in 1968. Georgian fronted, it has several graceful Venetian windows. Inside there is an 18th century staircase and in the south-east corner is a panelled room whose fireplace and decoration may have come from an earlier building of c.1620 on the same site. The house is surrounded by fine trees, including an oak tree planted by King George VI to mark his visit to the Essex Show which was held here in 1948; this tree is now in the garden of a house built in the grounds of the Hall. The Hall is associated with Richard Baker who built it between 1750 and 1789 when he was Lord of the Manor. He died in 1827 when the estate devolved upon his nephew William Wingfield who assumed the name Wingfield-Baker. In 1880 his son Digby Hanmer Wingfield inherited the estate. His succession coincided with the Great Depression in farming in Essex. Repairs to the sea wall at Shellhaven cost £30,000 and this effectively ruined the estate. Wingfield may have gambled away what remained of his inheritance but he raised a £50,000 mortgage in trust for his friend and brother officer Thomas Whitmore whom he nominated his executor and residuary legatee. Even before Wingfield's death in 1884 Thomas Whitmore was effectively running the estate. The Whitmores hailed originally from Shropshire where in 1780 an ancestor Thomas Whitmore was the first person for whom a table service in the now familiar Willow Pattern was made by Thomas Turner of Caughley. Thomas Whitmore was given a miniature Willow Pattern plate on a gold cravat pin to mark the occasion.

Orsett Show began in 1841; it was first held in the field behind the Hall. A new series of shows started in 1895 after a gap of a number of years and the Show's 50th anniversary was celebrated in 1956.

Further along the Brentwood Road near Bulphan stands the 15th century building, c.1420, of Appleton's Farm. This is a very attractive timber-framed hall house with gabled and jettied cross wings. The hall had an upper floor and chimney inserted in 1632 and both the hall and the east and west wings have king post roofs. Beside it is the Plough House Motel, Plough House being the 20th century name of Appleton's. In the grounds are two arches which came from the entrance to Christopher Shiner's Grays Carnegie library of 1903 which was demolished in 1971. The banqueting hall is a barn which came from Demington, near Diss in Norfolk. It was re-erected here in the 1970s. The dining hall is distinguished by wood panelling which is of Spanish origin. Note the carving of the Royal Arms of Leon and Castile, depicted by lions and castles. There are fox hunting trophies on the walls which came from Orsett Hall, one commemorating a hunt from Cranham Springs to the Dog and Partridge in 1911.

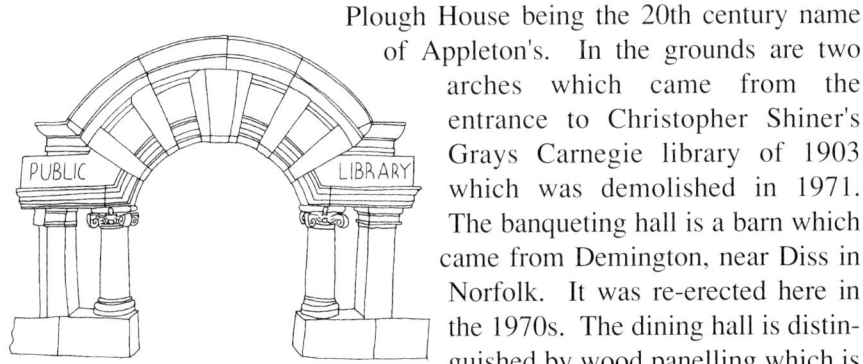

Entrance Arch from Grays Carnegie Library

Immediately behind Appleton's is Garlesters, on the old Brentwood Road. This was built in the 16th century or earlier and is a two-storey building with two gabled dormer windows. It has been extensively restored. Beside it are the remains of a moat.

On the edge of the area next to the Southend railway line is Barnards Farm

- a red brick 18th century building.

Bulphan (sometimes spelt Bulvan and other variants) takes its name from the "van" or fen on which it stands. The Domesday survey shows that it belonged to the Abbey of Barking. The 15th century church of St. Mary is built of flint and rubblestone; there was a major restoration in 1874/5. The south porch has some fine wood carving of Tudor roses and evangelistic symbols. Inside the door is a panel depicting the Royal arms of the first Hanoverian period (1714-1801); there is another depiction of these arms on the reverse. The fine oak screen was not designed for its present position but its 15th century origin is unknown. There is modern glass in the north east window of the nave in memory of Rev. Theodore Alphonse Teitelbaum, Rector 1903-1946. At the west end stands the impressive belfry constructed entirely of heavy timber. In 1981 the tower floor was relaid and covered with wooden blocks rescued from an old post office which was being demolished in Leeds.

Further along Fen Lane is Brandon Hall, the former Rectory, in Victorian Gothic red brick.

Church Lane leads back across the fenland towards Orsett. On the western edge of the fen, at the junction with Conway's road, is Conway's Farm which has a hipped roof and a central door with panelled pilasters from the early 18th century. Further along is Lorkins Farm. This is one of the oldest houses in the district, originating in the 15th century. It appears on Chapman and Andre's map of 1777 as Moores in the Clay. It is still most attractive with its gabled dormers and jettied cross-wing.

Conways Road leads to Orsett village. Orsett may get its name from the Saxon words "or" for water and "sett" for place or from iron working for which there is evidence in the area. To the east, down Prince Charles Avenue, is a gabled 18th century house with the unusual name The Bothy - originally the name of a building in which labourers lodged. Some of its timbers have been carbon dated to the 13th century. To the west on one corner of Maltings Lane (a name linked to the preparation of malt for home brewing, as at Aveley) is Larkin's Corner, a late 15th century timber-framed cottage with exposed timber work partly pargetted and weatherboarded. On the opposite south-east corner is a long building, Vine House and Church Row; this has a couple of trap doors at street level which gives the clue to the fact that this was the building in which the malting took place. The brewer himself lived in the house at the other end.

Ahead is the Whitmore Arms whose inn sign carries the arms of Lord of the Manor, Sir Francis Whitmore, who died in 1962 at the age of ninety. It was formerly the George and before that, the Dog and Gun inn, which gives its name to Gun Alley next to it. Beyond Gun Alley is Birch Cottage, an attractive 17th century thatched building with a jettied and gabled 16th century cross-wing to the south which has exposed timber framing. Part of the remainder is pargetted. Further along Rectory Road is the Congregational chapel of 1843. There is a stained glass window to W.O.Watt, dairy farmer of Heath Place.

Opposite the Whitmore Arms on the corner of High Road is no.2, originally Anson's school in Georgian days. Edward Anson's school was founded under his will of 1776. It opened in 1785, transferring to a new building in 1850 next to the National School with which it merged in 1896. Next door to no.2 is The Limes, an 1820s tall square building. It was built by a pupil of Anson's school, Wm. Archer, and known as Archer's Folly because he did not like his first attempt, so pulled it down and started again. The Limes also became a school in 1858.

On the south side of the High Road, no.13 was the post office and no.15 the butcher's of late 16th century date with the slaughterhouse behind it. Opposite is the parish church of St. Giles and All Saints. The church is entered through a Norman doorway. On the east jamb are no less than three scratch dials. The church is unusual in having two chancels, the first of which dates from about 1150. Today's chancel dates from about 1330 and the fine east window is also of that date. The screen between the nave and the chancel is modern and was made by Comper in 1911 from the timbers of H.M.Frigate "Pique" in which a local man, Admiral Charles Wright Bonham, served as a midshipman in the 19th century. The screens north and south of the chancel were designed by Sir Charles Nicholson in memory of Violet Whitmore, Sir Francis Whitmore's first wife.

Scratch Dial

The second chancel was built about 1500. It contains two Westmacott memorials to members of the Baker family and a notable collection of thirteen hatchments. There is a fourteenth in the vestry under the tower for the wife of the Rev. Usko. He was born in Prussia in 1760 and served this parish for 33 years. Under the perpendicular west window with glass by Kempe is an Italian 18th century sculpture.

Next to the church is the brick building which used to be the Crown inn; it still bears its sign bracket on the front. At the back is a chimney stack with the date 1674 and the initials IDM. Despite appearances this is actually a timber-framed building. Next door is a neat Georgian building with semi-circular-topped windows. Further along is the Foxhound where the game of quoits was popular in the 1900s. In the public bar hangs the Taylor Walker shield of 1912 which was last won in 1927. There is also an explanation of the game.

Beyond the Foxhound on the corner of Pound Lane are the village lock-up and pound. The lock-up is a small wooden building whose barred windows have been boarded up. Built in the 1700s, it was last used as a prison in 1848. For a long time it served as a henhouse before being erected on its present site in 1938. Pound Lane leads down to the junction with Maltings Lane where to the east lies early 16th century Old Hall Farmhouse which in its older parts is jettied and timbered. Hereabouts were the osier beds which supplied the filters for the first sewage system for the village which was pioneered by Col. Whitmore. Here too were the Orsett basket works which he started after the first world war for disabled ex-servicemen. It provided employment until about 1936. The wooden huts were later moved to the Orsett Fruit Farm on the road to Horndon.

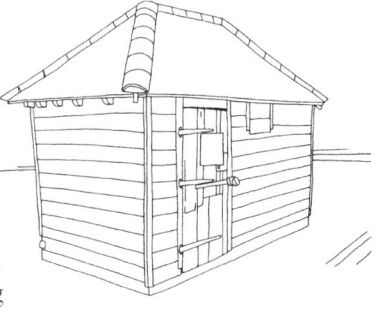

Orsett Lock - up

Behind is the site of Bishop Bonner's Palace. Bonner (1500-1569) was Bishop of London in the time of Mary Tudor and was blamed for the martyrdom of many Protestants, including Thomas Higbed of Horndon-on-the-Hill. The site has not been proved but it is a large circular moated enclosure with a rectangular bailey to the north. The house platform is of imported Thanet sand, perhaps from the upper denehole shafts at Orsett's Hangman's Wood. Plenty of medieval tile has been found in the area. It may have been the Bishop's hunting lodge: hunting, it is conjectured, went on at Stock where there was, until the 19th century, an outlying part of Orsett parish, which today is Crondon Park, a mile to the north-west of Stock.

Rowley Road leads to School Lane and the village school of 1848 and 1850. Opposite the school is Orsett Hospital. The hospital has its origins in the Union Workhouse of 1838. A new building was erected in 1870 which became a hospital during the first and second world wars. Work began on the rebuilding of the hospital in 1961 and it was developed and extended throughout the 1960s. The accident unit was closed in 1992 and some services moved to Basildon Hospital, as did the maternity unit in 1993.

Further along High Road is Finches, with the Whitmore arms on it in stone. This was where the Orsett wheelwright, William Finch, plied his trade. At one time it was a school. Standing back to the north of the High Road, in a small park on the corner of Fen Lane, is Orsett House. It actually faces north (the side farthest from the High Road) where the main road from Horndon to Aveley used to run via Maltings Lane. There is a ha-ha on this side separating the house and garden from the park. This fine three-storey brick building was erected in 1740 by Capt. Samuel Bonham. Inside are pedimented doorways and decorated borders to the ceilings. In the 19th century it became the Orsett Boarding Academy and in the 20th it was converted into apartments. Capt. Bonham was a successful slave trader. Despite his profession, he was highly respected, becoming churchwarden of Ratcliff Stepney in 1727. The trade was very lucrative despite heavy losses. For example, in 1733 in the "Sarah" galley, he traded goods for gold, elephants' teeth and 408 slaves but, by the time they reached Jamaica, only 167 slaves survived. Bonham died in 1745 and was buried in the churchyard at Orsett.

Along the road towards Baker Street is Slades Hold (now nos. 93-97). This is an 18th century terrace on a timber framework which was the original Orsett Poorhouse before the Union Workhouse was built. It was restored and thatched like the original in 1940. Near the crossroads is Mill House with Baker Street windmill behind it. The smock mill itself is known to have been insured in 1796; it was working up to 1912 and has been partially restored. The brick base of the octagonal mill is two storeys high. Weatherboarded Mill House is 15th or 16th century in origin. The surround and bracketed hood to the door in the centre were added later.

In the lane to the north opposite the King's Arms is a tall building which, though quite different in style, is contemporary with Slades Hold. Farther along Fen Lane on its northern arm on the flat expanse of Orsett Fen, stands Poplars Farm in 17th century style. Formerly Great Wellhouse Farm, it is plaster rendered with an assymetric facade belying its early 19th century doorcase and windows.

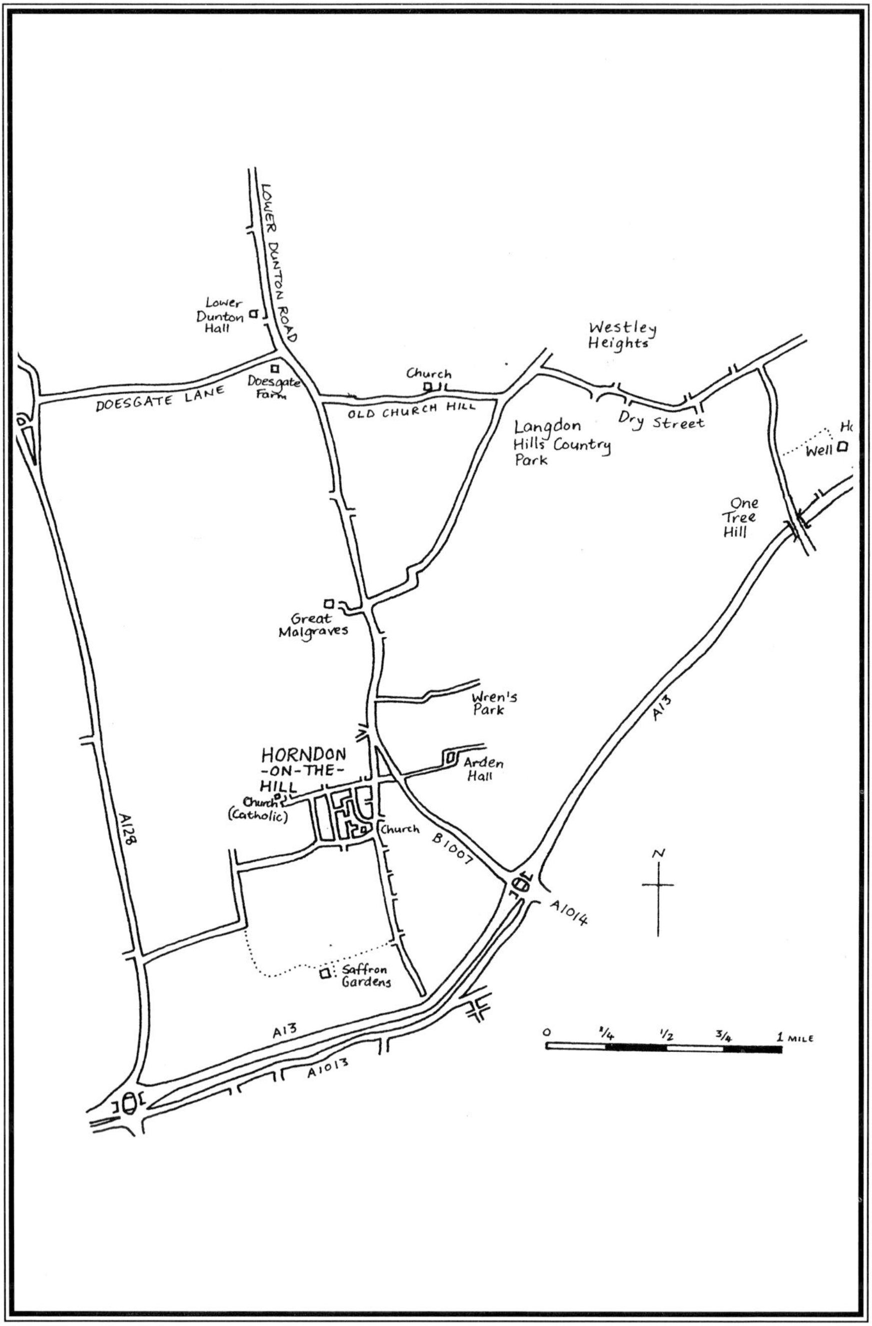
LOWER DUNTON ROAD
Lower Dunton Hall
Westley Heights
DOESGATE LANE
Doesgate Farm
Church
OLD CHURCH HILL
Langdon Hills Country Park
Dry Street
Well
One Tree Hill
Great Malgraves
Wren's Park
HORNDON -ON-THE- HILL
Arden Hall
Church (Catholic)
Church
B1007
A128
A13
A1014
N
Saffron Gardens
A13
A1013
0 1/4 1/2 3/4 1 MILE

The Highlands

The highest point in Thurrock (118 metres) is reached on Westley Heights in the Langdon Hills Country Park. Exploration of this part of Thurrock begins at the Orsett Cock roundabout. To the north-east is Barrington's Farm which has a 17th century chimney stack. The frontage is in 19th century brick which has been painted. To the south-west of the farmhouse aerial photography by the R.A.F. in 1946 discovered a complex double-ditched enclosure which was excavated in the late 1970s before it was destroyed by the building of the dual carriageway of the A13. Pottery and several Roman kilns were found. The Southend bound carriageway at this point was the scene of a crash by a North American P51B Mustang in 1944.

The A1013 towards Stanford passes Flight Hill where there was an airfield during the Great War followed by an air taxi service. At the roundabout where the A1013 meets the A1014, the Horndon bypass (B1007) goes to the north. Arden Hall stands out away to the east, an early 18th century house four square, three storeys high. An outbuilding on the eastern side has been shown to be part of a 15th century house. The dovecote to the south in red brick was put up in the 18th century.

North of Arden Hall is Wrens Park, a late 17th/early 18th century building, timber framed and roughcast in part. The next place of note is Great Malgraves at the end of a drive on the left hand side. This is a 16th century building, since enlarged and irregular in outline. Malgraves was one of the original manors of Horndon: Arneulph Malgrave is mentioned in 1200. The road now goes uphill past several of the Plotland bungalows which are still a feature of the Langdon Hills area. The Plotlands originated in speculative development in the 1890s following the decline in agriculture. On the left is Goldsmiths, once the home of Sir Joseph Dimsdale, Lord Mayor of London in 1901. Opposite is an area called The Park which was the site of an archaeological dig where Iron Age pottery was discovered. From the top of the hill the plain of Thurrock stretches out below with the Queen Elizabeth Bridge in the distance and Canary Wharf on the horizon. Nearly all of Thurrock can be glimpsed from vantage points in the Country Park. In his book published in 1772, the agricultural author Arthur Young writes,

"Near Horndon on the summit of a vast hill one of the most astonishing prospects to be beheld, breaks almost at once upon one of the dark lanes. Such a prodigious valley..... appears beneath you, that it is past description. Nothing can exceed it, unless that which Hannibal exhibited to his troops when he bade them behold the glories of the Italian plains!".

The boundary of Thurrock with its neighbour Basildon follows ancient field boundaries and so parts of Westley Heights and One Tree Hill, which make up the Country Park, are in each district. The Country Park has its origins in the concern felt at indiscriminate Plotland development in the 1920s. The Park began by the purchase by Essex County Council in 1930 of 60 acres around the summit of the Langdon Hills. This has resulted in the preservation of one of the most attractive parts of the Thurrock landscape.

Vange Well no.5

There is an interesting ruin near the foot of One Tree Hill near Hovels farm in Fobbing. It can be reached by taking the footpath downhill from opposite the car park adjacent to the Information Room. Spring water with medicinal properties (analysis showed it to contain 495 parts per 100,000 of Magnesium Sulphate) was discovered on Hovels Farm in 1899. It was not until 1919, when a Mr Cash retired as licensee of the Angel, Islington, and found such water on land he had purchased nearby, that the water became commercially available. The press took up the story of the Vange Water Co. and dubbed the area "The Vale of Health" in 1924. Its fame was, however, short lived and a small concrete and brick building in the style of a Grecian temple is all that remains. On the portico was inscribed "Vange Well no.5"; one or two of the other wellheads can still be made out.

Old Church Hill goes westwards down from the top of the Langdon Hills. It passes on the left the Old Rectory in 19th century red brick. On the right is another red brick building from an earlier age. This is the former church of St. Mary the Virgin and All Saints. It dates from the early 16th century and was carefully restored as a private residence by Robert Mill in 1975.

Inside over the chancel arch is a painting of the Royal Arms of the Stuarts and the date 1660. There is an inscription, doubtless to celebrate the Restoration, from Proverbs ch.24 v.21, "My son, fear thou the Lord and the King, and meddle not with them that are given to change". Towards the bottom of the hill on the right are the remains of the barbed wire fence and hutments associated with a prisoner of war camp from the second world war which was situated near the water tower at the top of the hill.

On the corner of Lower Dunton Road and Doesgate Lane, which leads to Bulphan, is Doesgate Farm. This is a 17th century weatherboarded timber-framed house very much as it must have looked 300 years ago. Lower Dunton Hall with a mansard roof, to the west of Lower Dunton Road, is in 18th century brick: it probably encloses an earlier building and has a late 19th century porch on which are carved the initials KC and the date 1898. Nearby is a pair of 19th century yellow brick cottages.

To the south on its prominent hill is Horndon-on-the-Hill, now a Conservation Area. The name is given in Domesday as Horninduna. There must have been an Anglo-Saxon mint hereabouts. The evidence for this rests on a unique penny now in the British Museum which was found in a hoard of 11th century coins at a site near St. Mary Hill church in the City of London in 1774. The coin is of the reign of Edward the Confessor and was minted between 1056 and 1059; the name Hornidune appears on the reverse.

Horndon Penny c.1057

The High Road branches off the B1007 Horndon bypass to the west. The first turning on the right is Hillcrest Road; at its western end at its junction with Oxford Road is the Roman Catholic church of 1938. Hereabouts the Oxford Medical Mission was established by Dr. Stansfield in 1900; he purchased 23 acres of land for a camp for boys from Bermondsey who were so poor they had to walk the whole 26 miles from where they lived. The area became known as The Priory. A photograph of 1907 shows one of the camp officers, Geoffery Fisher, who later became Archbishop of Canterbury.

Mill Lane, as its name suggests, leads to the remains of Horndon windmill.

This may be approached by way of a gated path beside the churchyard extension or from Francis Close. It was a post mill; all that is left from its demolition in 1917 is part of the round house and the cross-trees of the early 19th century building.

The church is dedicated to St. Peter and St. Paul. It is predominantly Early English in style. The bell-tower with its broach spire stands independently inside the nave on a massive oak structure which was made in the 15th century and restored at the beginning of the 20th century. On the south wall just inside the door is a memorial to Thomas Higbed, a Protestant martyr who lived in the village, who was burned at the stake in Horndon in 1555. Foxe includes him in his "Book of Martyrs" where he tells of the activities of Bishop Bonner, the then Bishop of London who may have had a palace at Orsett (see The Fenland). On the chancel floor are memorial slabs complete with coats of arms for members of the Kingsman family, one of whom was a trustee of Palmer's school. Beside the altar is a floor slab in memory of Anne Sandford whose age is given as 303 years. On the north wall of the sanctuary is a memorial to Daniel Caldwell who died in 1634. His widow erected the memorial which contains these verses:-

> *Take gentle Marble, to thy Trust*
> *And keep Unmixt, this sacred dust.*
> *Grow moist sometimes, that I may see*
> *Thou weepst in sympathy with me.*
> *And when by him I here shall sleepe,*
> *My ashes also, safely keepe.*
> *And from rude hands preserve us both, untill*
> *We rise to Syon Mount from Horndon Hill.*

There is a lectern which is a fine example of the Arts and Crafts Movement. It was made in 1899 by the Guild of Handicrafts to the design of the church restorer Charles Robert Ashbee.

On the outside of the church on a corner of the east window arch is a carved stone corbel known as the "Horndon Beauty". One gravestone of particular interest is on the west side of the footpath. It records Thomas Mann "Many years ashman of this parish" d. 1838, aged 85. The trade of potash making was widely spread throughout Essex. The nearest to Horndon was Potash

Hill (see The Fenland). Potash was often used for manure and also to make a form of water softener used by housewives. The trade declined when soap became cheaper. In the detached graveyard behind its iron railings north west of the church is the grave of Philip Conrad Vincent "Designer and inventor of the legendary Vincent motorcycles"; he died in 1979, aged 71.

There are a number of buildings of interest along the High Road whose name however changes as you go down the hill to South Hill, Pump Street and Horndon Road. This long village street is reached from the church by a passage-way variously known as the Gobble-shute or The Square. Along it is well-head machinery in the form of a cast-iron wheel mechanism c.1830. On the right fronting South Hill is the Woolmarket. This building has survived from the 16th century when Horndon was a centre for the wool trade. Two fairs were held in June and July up to a hundred years ago and the custom was revived in the 1980s. The ground floor was once an open market hall. Thurrock Council restored the building in 1969/70 to the design of local architect John Graham, for use as a local Arts Centre. On the left is a yellow brick building which at first sight appears to be c.1820 and continues along the full length of The Square, but buildings of several earlier dates lie hidden within, such as a small 15th century timber-framed house and an 18th century enlargement. Down the High Street to the north is early 18th century Halls Row, mansard roofed and once four terraced houses. Over the road is a thatched cottage which has been renovated following a fire on Guy Fawkes' night in 1985.

On the opposite side of the road from the Woolmarket are two houses of note. Eighteenth century Hill House to the right has a typical panelled door under a hood. High House to the left has a date on it, 1728 and the initials WK. The porch here is pedimented and the fine brick front is embellished with a parapet. Behind the brick frontage is a 17th century structure. The coach arch has curved panelled doors probably of a later date. The building on the corner of Orsett Road, The Stores, is built from three 500-year-old cottages in an L-plan. The upper floor is jettied over the road at the side. The double-fronted shop window is a 19th century one. Next door two more cottages have been joined together since they were built in the 16th century.

The Bell inn is one of the oldest in south east Essex; the front of the inn is

18th century work but along the jettied north wall is some fine exposed 15th century timber framing. The archway has its own roof separate from that of the inn; next to it, and now part if the premises, is a jettied building which was probably built at the same time as the medieval archway. In the reign of George III the inn was a staging post for the London coach which went by way of Orsett (q.v.). A four-horsed coach called "The Perseverance" called to collect travellers when the fare to Aldgate was 2s 6d (12 1/2p). Hanging up inside the inn are many hot cross buns - one for every year since 1900, when new publican Jack Turner celebrated his arrival by hanging up a bun. To keep up the sequence one or two were made in concrete as a wartime economy. A close look at the inn sign shows there are words inscribed on the bell:-

Vivo Voco   *I call the Living*
Mortuos Plango   *I toll for the Dead*
Fulgura Frango   *I shiver the Lightning*

Opposite the Bell, Gladstone Villas were put up in 1886. Nearby is The Old House, once the vicarage, built largely in the 17th century with an irregular shape which includes a mezzanine floor. On the other side of the hill is Grices; the north section is 18th century, the centre 16th century and the south 18th century again. As a result it has no less than four gabled roofs. On the western slope of the hill is a thatched cottage. The Gables in Pump Street is almost opposite where the pump used to be; it was formerly called Myrtle Cottage. This is a late 17th century timber-framed house gabled to the south. At the foot of the hill is a group of 18th century cottages: nos. 10, 11 and 12 Pump Cottages have a mansard roof along the terrace.

Beyond the cottages is the turning on the right which leads to Saffron Gardens. The name, like Saffron Walden, refers to the cultivation of Saffron, the yellow colouring matter obtained from a species of crocus. Norden's map of Essex (1584) shows a house was there at that time; later maps, such as Ogilby and Morgan (1678) and John Warburton (1749) refer to it as Cantis. There is a Sun Fire Insurance sign on the west wall, no.59229 which can be dated to 31 Nov. 1732. The Sun Fire Insurance Co. was founded in 1710; firemen would only put out a fire if the house was insured by their company, hence the need for an identification sign. The idea of insuring against fire was started by Nicholas Barbon after the Great

Fire of London in 1666. Part of the original house can be seen in the L-shaped plan, timber-framed with typical dormer windows. Modification in the 18th century added the french windows and the bays with hipped roofs on the south front. In an upstairs oak-panelled room with its original wood dowels and carved overmantel is a fireplace, discovered in 1914, which has been painted over. On it the coat of arms of the Rich family can be made out. This was the house where Master Edward Rich was Queen Elizabeth's host when she visited Tilbury in 1588.

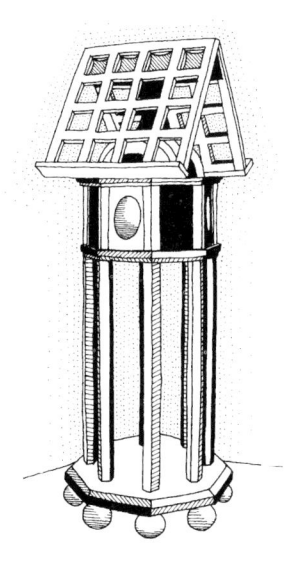

Lectern by
Charles Robert Ashbee

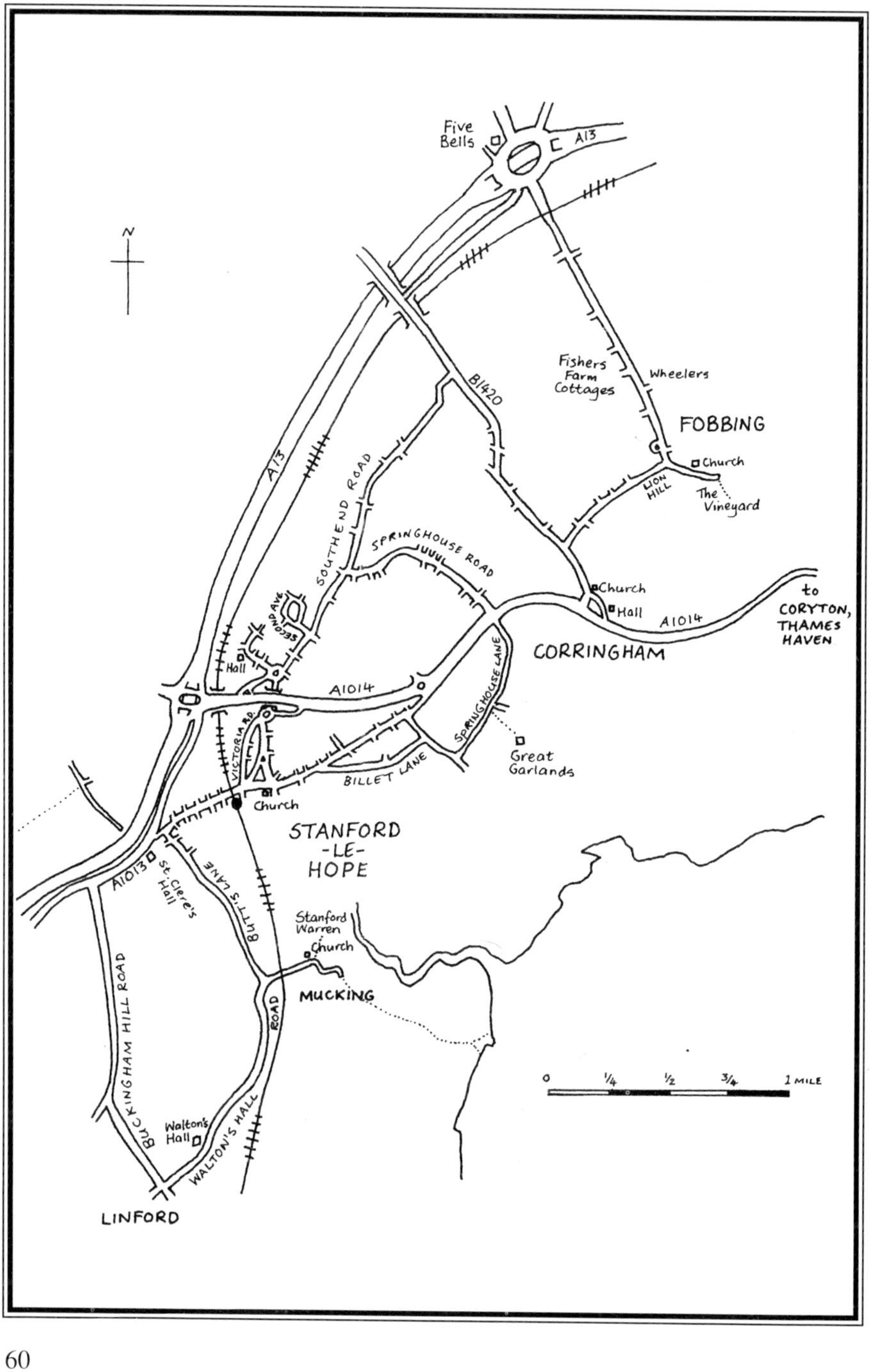
Five Bells
A13
N
A13
B1420
Fishers Farm Cottages
Wheelers
FOBBING
Church
LION HILL
The Vineyard
SOUTHEND ROAD
SPRINGHOUSE ROAD
SECOND AVE
Hall
Church
Hall
A1014
to CORYTON, THAMES HAVEN
CORRINGHAM
A1014
VICTORIA RD.
SPRINGHOUSE LANE
Great Garlands
BILLET LANE
Church
STANFORD -LE- HOPE
A1013
St. Clere's Hall
BUTTS LANE
Stanford Warren
Church
MUCKING
ROAD
BUCKINGHAM HILL ROAD
0
1/4
1/2
3/4
1 MILE
Walton's Hall
WALTON'S HALL
LINFORD

Eastern Approaches

To the south of Saffron Gardens, lying back from the main road, is St. Clere's Hall. This began life as New Jenkyns (see below); the older part to the east may contain the original late 17th century house. The two-storey Georgian brick building with a later parapet was built in 1735 by James Adams, Clerk of the Stables to George II. He called it Adamsley; later it became The Rookery - it lies by Rookery Corner. Adams has an unusual tombstone in Stanford churchyard (see below). The name of the house was changed again by William Wilson in 1934 after he bought it following his sale of the old St. Clere's (Sinclairs on some old maps) to the Bata Shoe Company for the development of their new factory at East Tilbury. The name St. Clere comes from William de Sancto Claro whose name appears in the 13th century. William "Have a go" Wilson died in 1975: in 1962 he started a special award with Essex Police for people who "have a go" when they see a crime being committed. He did just that himself when he tackled a burglar in 1974! On the front of the building is an 18th century fire insurance sign of the Hand-in-Hand Fire Office. The drawing room has a fine oak fireplace dated 1581; it bears the arms of Pigott and a latin inscription. An unusual feature is an elevating partition which enables the room to be enlarged at will.

Buckingham Hill Road leads to Linford. Here was an abortive attempt to build a thriving residential estate in the 19th century. The roads are named after English counties. Some of the original Victorian buildings can still be seen; most have made way for 20th century development. The name Linford was coined for this estate in a curious way. The original name for the area was Muckingford. It seems that the developers were not enamoured of the first part of the name and so tried a latin equivalent (limus = slime or mud), which a printer's error in the advertisement made Linford.

The road from Linford to Stanford and Mucking is called Walton's Hall Road. Walton's was a Manor of Mucking; there are earlier than 17th century traces in the present Walton's Hall farmhouse of c.1835 on the north side of the road. There is a farm museum here with a collection of agricultural and domestic items dating back over two hundred years housed in the

17th century barn. A number of rare breeds are on show. From the car park there is a view of the escarpment to the north where, from 1965 to 1978, there was an outstanding archaeological dig to uncover the remains of two thousand years of Thurrock's past.

Apart from the name "Mucca's place" the evidence for the extensive Saxon settlement here is entirely archaeological. 1959 was a vintage year for crop marks. The early summer drought hastened the ripening of cereals growing on shallow soils such as usually overlie gravel, but those plants which had their roots in the deeper and so damper soil which had accumulated in ancient ditches remained greener far longer. It was this contrast between green and gold which made it possible for the layout of the ancient features to be seen and photographed from the air. Subsequent rescue excavation of the site before the gravel was extracted was carried out by the Department of the Environment with the help of members of the Thurrock Local History Society and an international team of students and experts under the leadership of Margaret Jones. This was the first time in Britain that such an extensive and complex cropmark site had been fully excavated, enabling archaeologists to discover how communities from the Bronze Age to the medieval period had used the same landscape. The excavation made a particular contribution to Anglo-Saxon studies by revealing sunken huts (grubenhauser) and cemeteries associated with the earliest phase of Anglo-Saxon immigration in the 5th century A.D. There is an exhibit about the site and replicas of some of the finds in Thurrock Museum. The originals are in the British Museum.

Mucking Brooch
Fifth Century

At the junction with Butts Lane, Mucking Wharf Road leads to the village of Mucking. The church of St. John the Baptist is now in private hands. Its three ancient bells, one of which dated 1665 has the imprint on it of coins of the period, are now in the care of St. Clement's church, West Thurrock. Mucking church was largely rebuilt in the 19th century but parts remain from the 13th century. To this period belongs the "Green Man" fertility symbol on a carved capital in the south aisle arcade. In the south chapel is an alabaster monument to Elizabeth Downes who died in 1607. She was four times married; the first of her husbands was Eugeny Gatton who owned the farm called Jenkyns. Her second husband was Thomas Gill who took on the Jenkyns estate. About a century later, there being no male heir, the estate came into the hands of two sisters who decided to divide their inheritance. One took the original house calling it Old Jenkyns while the other built another and called it New Jenkyns. Old Jenkyns has been variously identified with Butts Farm, near to New Jenkyns and which was demolished in 1900, and with Mucking Hall near the church. Thomas Gill, together with his son Ralph, was Keeper of the Lions in the Tower of London in 1591. This collection originated in a gift to Henry III in 1235 of three leopards by Frederick II, Holy Roman Emperor; this was a reference to Henry's Royal Arms. At one time there were elephants, besides over 100 rattlesnakes. The zoo was closed in 1835 immediately after one of the lions attacked some members of the garrison.

Mucking "Green Man"

At the church gate is the old schoolhouse dated 1855 next door to the substantial Victorian rectory. Opposite the church stands the Hall, a tall 17th century three-storey building with an early 19th century facade. To the south-east is a rebuilt house which was once the Crown inn. Overlooked by the churchyard is the Stanford Warren nature reserve managed by Thurrock Wildlife Society on behalf of the Essex Wildlife Trust. It is the site of the largest reed bed in Essex. Footpath no.38 leads across a causeway to Stanford Warren and Stanford Marshes, an area of open land to the south of Stanford-le-Hope. Hereabouts is one of only a few riverside areas in Thurrock which are accessible to the public. A footpath leads to Stanford beach past Mucking creek.

It was the Rev. Palin who pointed out in "Stifford and its Neighbourhood" in 1871 that the name of Stanford-le-Hope has been as much disputed as Homer's birthplace. The most likely meaning has been deduced starting from Domesday where this area is called Hasinghebroc or the "low marshy ground of Hassa's people". Enclosures of fen areas in south-east England are known as hopes, the nearest being beyond Fobbing Vineyard (q.v.) and

O.E. Hop possesses the same topographical meaning as Broc. Hence the Domesday name becomes adjusted to the "low marshy ground with a stone ford". It has nothing to do with the River Thames. The original name is preserved in the name of the stream by the station and in the name of Hassingbrook Hall. At the time of Domesday the majority of the land was held by Ralf, son of Turold of Rochester who appears in the Bayeux tapestry.

In the church dedicated to St. Margaret of Antioch, Norman, Early English, Decorated and Perpendicular styles can be found. It was greatly restored in 1877-8; the tower and west front were added in 1883. There are several monuments to the Fetherstons of Hassingbrook Hall whose coat of arms included charges of a feather and molets which are a pun on the name. In the churchyard beyond the west end is an interesting half-barrelled tomb, decorated with a gruesome display of bones. The canopy carving at the back is an example of a baldacchino. The inscription in the grand manner is to James Adams who built the house now known as St. Clere's Hall (see above), dying in 1765.

Near the junction of Southend Road and Victoria Road in an area with some examples of Victorian housing of 1882 lies the evidence of the presence here of the Peculiar People. This was a revivalist movement of born-again christians which flourished in the 19th century in Essex. They believed in divine healing and refused to accept medical intervention. Their name comes from the Book of Deuteronomy ch.14 v.2, "the Lord hath chosen thee to be a peculiar people unto himself, above all the nations that are upon the earth". Their first church in Stanford was no.41a Southend Road; the next church was nearby and behind it in Victoria Road is the Evangelical church of 1924 - they became part of the Union of Evangelical Churches in 1956.

Hassingbrook Hall, now called Hassenbrook like the nearby school, can be found in the area beyond the A1014 (The Manorway) where the streets are named after English composers. Cuthbert Fetherston rebuilt it in 1607 but it has been considerably altered by modern brickwork. The brick garden walls are original and are decorated with small niches possibly used for small bee-skips. In the south wall is a four-centred gateway surmounted by a triangular pediment almost invisible in modern development. Matthew Fetherstonhaugh of Featherstone Castle in Northumberland inherited the property in 1746, the year in which he bought Uppark near Petersfield in Sussex. The story of the connection with Lord Nelson has already been told (see Polwicks in The Tilburys).

In Second Avenue stands a cedar tree which is the subject of a preservation order. It stands in what was once the garden of Moore Place. In 1909 Captain James Petavel together with his wife and children and a few friends set up a Christian Socialist colony. An essential part of the scheme was the elimination of money as a means of exchange and they formed a limited company called "Production for Use Industries". The experiment was short lived: in 1915 Petavel was on his way to India at the invitation of the poet Rabindranath Tagore. In 1930 Moore Place was purchased by "The Wayfarers Benevolent Association" but in 1960 this finally gave way to those urban pressures which Captain Petavel sought to escape, and the house was demolished for housing development.

Another name associated with Stanford-le-Hope is that of Joseph Conrad. Born Josef Teodor Korzeniowski in the Ukraine in 1857, Conrad lived in Stanford from 1896 to 1898. His parents were exiled Polish landowners; he himself went to sea for twenty years, becoming a captain in the British Merchant Navy. He came to Stanford to be near his friend Captain Hope through whom he had met his wife Jessie. The Conrads first rented a semi in what is now Victoria Road (it was called New Road until the 1897 Jubilee) - the number has not been established, but in her book on Conrad Jessie says, "it was a brand new twin villa at the end of the road running from the railway station". She has also recorded Conrad's instructions for his arrival at their new home: "I was to be ready dressed for the evening and take my ease in the drawing room three days after the arrival of the furniture; the new maid was to be instructed to answer his ring and show him into his room; the meal was to appear; he was to be shown to his study complete with bookshelves and all the neccessary paraphernalia, ready for the start next morning on a new masterpiece". He had written a suggested menu for his first dinner in his own house and had ended his letter with the command to "buy myself a pretty neglige for the mornings". When he arrived however, she forgot his instructions and rushed to the door; the evening was a complete disaster.

Cramped conditions led them to move to the farmhouse Ivy Walls off Billet

Lane. The present 1920s house replaced the one Conrad lived in. Whilst in Stanford he completed "Nigger of the Narcissus" and began "The Rescue". Conrad Road stands as a reminder of the novelist.

Beyond Ivy Walls, Rainbow Lane and Springhouse Lane lead to Great Garlands. In the flintwork of this Georgian house is a tablet which says "This house and stable built by Thomas Mashiter in 1753". At the gate is a stone inscribed, "Built by Thomas Mashiter 1874"; this refers to cottages in Broadhope Lane nearby, built by a descendant.

The Manorway leads down to the oil refineries of Shell and Mobil. They owe their existence to the "Petroleum Act" of 1871 which restricted the quantities of flammable material which could be taken up river to London. One event of note here previous to this was the last British Heavyweight Championship under bare-fisted rules. This took place by the sea wall at Thameshaven in 1862. Jem Mace and Tom King fought forty two rounds; Jem Mace was the winner, collecting a prize of about 400 gold sovereigns. Off the coast hereabouts used to stand Mucking lighthouse, at the end of a walkway out in the River Thames. It collapsed in 1964; Charles Dickens was probably describing the place when he wrote towards the end of "Great Expectations", "a little squat shoal-light, on open piles, stood crippled in the mud on stilts and crutches; and slimy stakes stuck out of the mud, and slimy stones stuck out of the mud, and red landmarks and tidemarks stuck out of the mud, and an old landing stage and an old flat roofless building slipped into the mud, and all about us was stagnation and mud".

In 1876 a private company was set up which became the London and Thameshaven Oil Wharves Ltd. Shellhaven may come from the Saxon "scylf" (a shelf or sandbank, beside which is a safe haven for tying up ships, cf. the Black Shelf in the Thames between West Thurrock and Grays) by confusion with "schyl" (shell); it appears as Shellhaven on Norden's map of 1610. A refinery was constructed here in 1914 by the Anglo-Saxon Petroleum Co. which became part of the Shell Group, whose emblem is a scallop shell, at "Shell"haven by coincidence.

Just as the 1871 Petroleum Act brought the oil companies, the 1875 Explosives Act eventually did the same for another industry. The Miners' Safety Explosive Co. established a factory on the marshes westward of the

Thameshaven oil jetty in 1890. In 1895 Kynoch & Co. of Birmingham bought 200-acre Borley Farm nearby for use as an explosives factory planned to cope with the anticipated war in South Africa. Near this factory a model village was built and named Kynochtown in 1899. During the 1914-18 war Kynochtown became one of the largest explosives factories, employing 6000 workers. The area was connected with Corringham by a light railway which used to bring people to work. The site of Corringham station can be visited and the line of the railway made out from footpath no.22 from Corringham to Fobbing beside the sports ground at the Fobbing end. After the war the industry died and by 1921 had closed down. Knochtown was taken over by Cory Bros. for a refinery and oil storage and renamed Coryton. Cory Bros. continued to support the community, as did the Vacuum Oil Co. (later Mobil Oil Co.) who purchased the site in 1950. In 1969 the villagers were told of the imminent closure of the Coryton community because of the need for refinery expansion. A fluid catalytic cracker complex now stands in its place beyond the roundabout at the end of The Manorway.

Back along The Manorway, Church Road, B1420 leads to old Corringham. The church of St. Mary has an impressive early Norman tower; the external walls contain herringbone rubble on the south side, probably of pre-conquest date. A couple of brasses are to be seen on the floor of the sanctuary. One c.1340 shows a demi-priest who seems to need a shave; the other is c.1460 and is thought to be that of Thomas Baud, Lord of the Manor. The north chapel is the de Baud chantry: it contains a marble bracket which is a fragment of the high altar reredos of St. Paul's cathedral which was demolished by enemy action in the 1939-45 war. St. Paul's connection with Corringham goes back to the year 1375 when Sir William de Baud obtained permission from the Dean and Chapter to enclose land. In return he promised to present them annually with one fat buck and one fat doe. The Rev. Samuel Stephenson was Rector from 1862 to 1887; a copy of his oratorio "Enoch's Prophesy" is in Thurrock Museum archives.

Beyond the church is Corringham Hall, an early 18th century brick building with an old mansard roof in which are three hipped dormer windows. Opposite the church is a group of timber-faced buildings whose early character has been retained despite modernisation. The Bull inn was mainly rebuilt in the 17th century but has a 15th century cross-wing. It was restored in 1974 by Charringtons. Hall Farm Cottages next door was originally 16th century, rebuilt in the 18th century and again in 1980. Bell House was built early in the 18th century. On the other side of the road is Bush House, a two storey building from the 16th century, weatherboarded over timber framing. The south wing may be a century earlier. The church is approached from the junction of Church Road and Fobbing Road where stands The Old School House, the first village school in Corringham (1840).

In Springhouse Road is the Village Hall. Outside it are several boundary posts which were found in 1963 at Oak Farm when the 400 year old house was being demolished. Carved on the sides of the posts are the names and initials of various landowners and the acreage of the land concerned. They were formerly used to mark the boundary between Stanford-le-Hope and Corringham. On one of them is chiselled "W.Eve 1839"; he farmed Manor Farm, North Ockendon; his son Frederick became a famous Victorian surgeon at St. Bartholomew's Hospital.

At the end of Fobbing Road is Lion Hill, on the north side of which is the White Lion. This is a timber-framed two-storey building possibly of 15th century date with a central hall and two cross-wings. In the public bar a game called Ring the Bull was once played. The support for the rope which held a ring on the end is still there. The skill in the game was to swing the ring onto a hook keeping the rope taut all the time.

On the outside of the inn is a plaque which commemorates the 600th anniversary of the Peasants' Revolt in 1981. A memorial to the original event is in the recreation ground: it takes the form of a metal sculpture by B.R.Coode-Adams and was re-erected here, at the wish of local residents, after being in a more prominent position. Local people were certainly involved in the Peasants' Revolt which followed the imposition of poll taxes in 1377, '79 and '81 to pay for the war against France during the Hundred Years War. One was Thomas Baker of Fobbing who led those who attacked the King's Messenger who came to Brentwood to enquire into a significant shortfall in the amount collected. Baker escaped when the uprising was suppressed but forty years later he returned to Fobbing where he was recognised, captured and judged to deserve the awful fate of being hung, drawn and quartered - virtually half-hanged, abdomen opened, and entrails shown to him and burnt before his eyes, and finally quartered with iron blades and his limbs exhibited at public draping points. Jack Straw, another supposed local leader, is probably a name like Jack Tar or Tommy Atkins; the better known Wat Tyler actually came from Kent.

The church is dedicated to St. Michael. The great west tower was used as a watch-tower and beacon in times of trouble. A small cannon ball was found in 1965 when the site for a new village hall was being excavated on land opposite the church. The ball may have been one from the Dutchman de Ruyter's attack in 1667. The porch doorway has the date 1734 on it and some contemporary carving. The oldest part of the church is the nave which is Saxon in origin; there is a blocked late Saxon window in the north wall. The south aisle has some early 16th century benches. In the chancel is an inscribed tablet written in Lombardic characters in Norman French of c.1350. The Royal Arms above the south door are from the third Hanoverian period (George IV). The crown above the central escutcheon came after 1816 when the electorate of Hanover was elevated to the dignity of a kingdom at the Congress of Vienna. At the west end is an old barrel organ which was restored in 1974; it plays hymn tunes.

The road leading downhill past the church is called Wharf Road and recalls the time when Fobbing Creek was a hive of activity. Footpath 143 leads to where the wharf used to be. The creek was dammed up after the floods of 1953. At the end of the road stands Fobbing Hall, a 16th century house, much modernised. The Manor of Fobbing was given by Henry VIII to Sir Thomas Boleyn, father of Anne and grandfather of Queen Elizabeth I. Opposite are Ship Cottages which were once the Ship inn. The original is 17th century but was rebuilt in the early 18th century and converted in 1975. Inside is a re-used roof beam which is reported to have the date 1564 on it. Coming back up the road, on the right hand side is a large wooden building similar to those used in Kynochtown. At the top are the remaining buildings and chimney of the early 19th century bakehouse, last used in 1929.

Footpath no.24 beside the Gardner Hall leads to The Vineyard which is recorded as early as 1539. Vineyards House was demolished in 1966 and the area is now a public open space on which is a beacon erected in 1988 to commemorate the Armada of 1588. The stretch of water at the foot was known as The Fleet, stretching from Fobbing Creek to the foot of Lion Hill.

Sailing barges used to anchor along this waterway. Beyond lay the enclosed lands known as the Hopes.

Next to the church stands the former rectory. It is dominated by the large Victorian wing but the original rectory can still be recognised as a most attractive house. It was built in the early 18th century in red and black brick with a parapet and an unusually high hipped roof in which are two hipped dormer windows. The porch is Victorian but encloses a Georgian panelled door. The name is now Pell House commemorating the Rev. John Pell, the inventor of the division sign in mathematics and joint designer with Sancroft of the calendar we use today. Married to a lady with the unusual name of Ithumaria and speaking several languages fluently, he was appointed to the Chair of Mathematics at Amsterdam University in 1643. Three years later he occupied a similar Chair at Breda. Cromwell appointed him to a personal lectureship in mathematics in 1652 and made him his representative in Zurich in 1654. For some obscure services to the Royalist Party he was made Rector of Fobbing (including also Pitsea and Basildon) in 1661.

On the other side of the High Road is an 18th century building with a pantiled roof and nearby is Prosbus Hall. The latter was first built in the 16th century but was refaced with brick in the 18th century. It is a two-storey house with attics; across the end of the old wing at the back is a 17th century chimney stack. The panelled door under a hood is Georgian. On the front of the building is a Sun fire insurance sign, no.87172 which can be dated to between 1740 and 1745.

Sun Fire Insurance Sign c.1742

Opposite the top of Lion Hill is Curtis Farm, a late 19th century building restored in 1983, behind which is a granary on staddle stones, weatherboarded in elm, in which a beam has been reported with the date 1837 on it. Further along the High road are several interesting buildings. Payne's Cottages are dated 1861 and Bay Cottages 1881. Copeland House is much older and has been dated to the last quarter of the 14th century, rebuilt in the early 19th century. Only two storeys high it has a gabled attic window. There was a model railway running round the garden in the 1960s. On the other side of the road is Wheeler's. A Rafe Wheeler was buried at Fobbing in 1585; the house is late 16th century. It is a hall house with two jettied wings under the same roof as the centre block, uncommon in this area and known as the Wealden type elsewhere. The extension on the south side is 17th century work. On the west side of the High Road are Fisher's Farm Cottages. The buildings comprise a hall, shed, barn and stable which belonged to a small yeoman farmer in the 15th century.

Marsh Lane leads to Nazewick and Fowler's marshes. Few grazing marshes survive on Thameside; this area is now a nature reserve managed by the Essex Wildlife Trust under the name Fobbing Marsh.

Where the Fobbing High Road meets the Five Bells roundabout is the easternmost boundary of Thurrock. In Tudor times the Five Bells inn was in the parish of Fobbing. There were formerly five bells in the tower of Fobbing church, three more being added in the 20th century. The parish rate book entry for 19 April 1838 reads, "Paid at Vange Bells for drinks for all walking the bounds".

Bibliography

Aldrich C.L. — History of the London, Tilbury and Southend Railway; E.V. Aldrich, 1946

Andree J. — An Account of the Tilbury Water; John Ellison, 1779

Astbury A.K. — Estuary (Land and water in the lower Thames basin);The Carnforth Press, 1980

Babbidge A. — Land of the Yielding Flood; Thurrock Borough Council, 1975

Barnes B. — Grays Thurrock (A pictorial History); Phillimore, 1988

Grays Thurrock Revisited; Phillimore, 1991

Barrett-Lennard T. — The families of Lennard and Barrett; 1908

Benton T. — Boldly from the marshes (A History of Little Thurrock and its people); Tony Benton & Thurrock Borough Council, 1992

Bingley R. — Fobbing (to be published)

West Tilbury (to be published)

Brooks H.E. — William Palmer and his School; Bentham, 1928

Carney T.J. — Thurrock in the Twenties; Thurrock Borough Council, 1990

The Story of Belhus (video); Thurrock Borough Council, 1992

Christy M. and Thrush, Mary — The Mineral Waters and Medicinal Springs of Essex; Essex Field Club, 1910

Collins E.J.T. — A History of the Orsett Estate; Thurrock Borough Council, 1978

Conrad, Jessie — Joseph Conrad and his Circle; Jarrolds, 1935

Conservation Area leaflets; Paul Shelley, Thurrock Borough Council

Dean, Doreen and Studd, Pamela — The Stifford Saga (1180-1980); 1980

Dolley R.H.M. — Anglo-Saxon Coins; Methuen, 1961 (ed.)

Edwards A.C and Newton K.C. — The Walkers of Hanningfield (Mapmakers); Buckland Publications Ltd., 1984

Essex Countryside

Essex Journal
Essex Review
Firmin, Jackie   Builders of Time (Orsett); 1993
Fobbing '81 600th Anniversary; Fobbing '81 Committee, 1981
   Forrester H.   The Timber-Framed Houses of Essex; The
                 Tindal Press, 1959
   Gotheridge I.   The Corringham Light Railway; Oakwood Press,
                 1985
   Grieve, Hilda   The Great Tide; Essex County Council, 1959
   Hardy H. and
   Ward C.   Arcadia for All (The Plotlands); Mansell, 1984
   Harrold C.   The Story of St. Clement's; Procter & Gamble Ltd.,
                 1992
   Hayston J.R.   250 years on (To commemorate the 250th anniver-
                 sary of the Trust Deed of Palmer's School); 1956
   Henshall T.A.S.   Ninety Years 1867-1957 (The story of Grays Co-
                 operative Society); 1957
   Hewett C.A.   The development of carpentry, 1200-1700 (An Essex
                 Study); David & Charles, 1969
Langdon Hills Country Park; Essex County Council, 1983
List of Buildings of Special Architectural and Historic Interest; Dept. of the
                 Environment, 1981
Local History Collection in Grays Library (catalogue in Local Studies
                 Section of Library)
   Maps   Chapman and Andre, 1777
                 Estate Maps (see Sparkes' Bibliography)
                 John Oliver, 1698
                 Norden & Speed, 1610
                 Ogilby & Morgan, 1678
                 Ordnance Surveys
                 Robert Norden, 1695
                 Seth Partridge, 1645
                 Tithe Awards, from 1837
   Matthews, Jean   Little Thurrock Church and Parish; 1970
   May D. le   History of Bulphan (typescript in Thurrock Museum
                 Archives), 1974
   McLean, Rita   The Downstream Dock (Tilbury); Thurrock Borough
                 Council, 1896

Miller, Molly   Safe in the Country (The experiences of a teacher at a Bulphan primary school 1938-1942); Stockwell, 1983
Morgan G.H.   Forgotten Thameside; The Thames Bank Publishing Co., 1951
Ormston J.M.   The Five Minute Crossing (Tilbury-Gravesend Ferries); Thurrock Local History Society, 1992
Palin W.   Stifford and its Neighbourhood, 1871
                       More about Stifford and its Neighbourhood, 1872
Panorama (Journal of Thurrock Local History Society: articles on local history and archaeology); Indices 1956-1989
Payne J.K.   The Corringham Chronicle; Phobinge Press, 1987
Pevsner N. and
Radcliffe, Enid   Buildings of England, Essex; Penguin, 1965.
Plotland Album   (The Story of the Dunton Hills Community); Basildon Development Corporation, 1983
Queen Elizabeth Slept Here; Thurrock Local History Society, 1988
Randall, Martha   Diary (transcript in Thurrock Museum Archives), 1861
Reaney P.H.   The Place Names of Essex; Cambridge University Press,935
Royal Commission on Historical Monuments (England). An Inventory of the Historical Monuments in Essex; H.M.S.O., vol. IV, 1923
Saunders A.   Stanford-le-Hope (A History of the Church and Village); 1988
Scott, Winifred   Coryton (The History of a Village); Mobil Oil Co. Ltd., 1982
Smith V.T.C.   Coalhouse Fort; 1985
Smith W.J.T. and
Worsley H.G.   Brasses of Thurrock and District; 1970
Smith, Wendy   An Historical look at Thurrock; Thurrock Borough Council, 1983
Sorrell M.   The Peculiar People; The Paternoster Press, 1979

Sparkes I.G.   Compilations of articles on Belhus, Corringham, Purfleet and Tilbury; 1963/4
                       The History of Thurrock (A Guide and

Thompson L.	Bibliography);1964 The Land that Fanns (told from its Parish Records); 1957 The Orsett Show; 1956 The Story of Mucking Church and Parish; 1962
Thurrock Gazette	
Thurrock in old picture postcards; Thurrock Borough Council, 1984	
Thurrock Museum and its Archives (by arrangement with the Museum Curator)	
Tilbury Fort Guide; English Heritage	
Tinworth W.M.	Saffron, Cider & Honey (A Town Trail of Horndon-on-the-Hill); The Horndon-on-the-Hill Society, 1985
Vellacott E.	Out of an Horrible Pit (West Thurrock); Excalibur Press, 1993
Victoria County History, Essex (especially vol. 8, 1983)	
Whitaker J.	Joseph Conrad at Stanford-le-Hope; Bream Press, 1978
Woollings, Barbara	Tales from God's Acre (Orsett); 1993
Wright B.	The British Fire Mark; Woodhead-Faulkener, 1982
Young A.	A six weeks tour; W.Strahan et al., 1772

People Index

Adams, James	61,64
Anson, Edward	47
Archer, Wm.	47
Ardalle, John	17,18
Artists - see Subjects/Groups index	
Aveley Band	6
Baker family	44,48
Barrett, Edward (Lord Newburgh)	7
Barrett, Thomas (Lord Dacre)	7
Barrett Lennard, Sir Thomas	8
Bata, Thomas	40
Baud, Thomas	67
Bingley, Randal	20,32
Boleyn, Sir Thomas	69
Bonham, Admiral	47
Bonham, Capt. Samuel	49
Bonner, Bishop	48,56
Bourchier, Sir Thomas	15
Brandon, Sir William	10
Brennan	31
Brett family	6
Brooks, Edmund	14,19
Brooks, Herbert	19
Brown, Capability	7
Bruyn, Sir Ingelram	10
Button, Zachariah	19,20
Caius, Dr.	34
Caldwell, Daniel	56
Cass, Sir John	35
Cedd, St.	36
Claro, William de Sancto	61
Clays, Sir John	19
Cook, Polly	26
Crammavill, Henry de	19
Davenant, Rev. Ralph	38

Dimsdale, Sir Joseph	53
Downes, Elizabeth	62
Durninge, John	19
Edwards W.H.	19
Fairfax	23,36
Feenan	31
Fetherston, Cuthbert	64
Fetherston family	64
Fetherstonhaugh, Matthew	64
Fetherstonhaugh, Sir Matthew	37
Finch, William	49
Fisher, Geoffery	55
Franklin, Benjamin	12
Freeman	19
Gatton, Eugeny	63
Gill, Thomas	63
Gomme, Bernard de	33
Gordon, General	33,38
Gourney, Sir Thomas	17
Graham, John	57
Grai, Henry de	21
Grantham, Nathaniel	15
Grantham, Kenwrick	19
Gurnett, Sir Henry	5
Hamilton, Sir Wm.	37
Hart, Emma	37
Hathe, J'Atte de	43
Haw Haw, Lord	24
Hayes, Rev.	15
Higbed, Thomas	48,56
Hogarth, John	19
Ingram	26,37
Jones, Margaret	62
Kellaway, John	36
King, Tom	66
Kings & Queens - see Subjects/Groups index	
Kingsman family	19,56
Knevynton, Ralph de	7

77

Lathum family	18
Loftus, Col.	37
Macdonald, Ramsay	31
Mace, Jem	66
Malgrave, Arneulph	53
Mann, Thomas	56
Mashiter, Thomas	66
Meeson	20
Mill, Robert	54
Nelson, Lord	37
Nevison, John	35
O'Shea, Kitty	12
Palin, Rev. Wm.	19,63
Palmer, William	19,23,25
Parnell	12
Peculiar People, The	64
Pell, Rev. John	70
Perchehay, Radulph	18
Petavel, Captain James	65
Prime, Thomas	6
Rich, Edward	59
Ruyter de	69
Saltonstall, Sir Richard	10
Sandford, Anne	56
Seabrooke family	23
Shiner, Christopher	21,22,45
Silverlock, James	17,19
Simmons, Rev.	19
Stansfield, Dr.	55
Sturgeon family	10
Teitelbaum, Rev.	46
Theobald family	23
Tillett, Ben	32
Turp, George	26
Turpin, Dick	35
Tyrrell	27
Usko, Rev.	48
Vincent, Philip Conrad	57

Watt W.O.	47
Watts, Jack	11
Wheeler, Rafe	71
Whitbread, Samuel	12
Whithwam, Rev.	39
Whitmore family	19,44,45,47,48
Wilson, William	61
Wingfield, Digby	43,44
Wingfield, William	44
Wingrove	12
Writers - see Subjects/Groups index	
Yamazaki, Kadzuo	27

Places Index

Aldgate School	35
Anson's School	47
Appleton's Farm	45
Archer's Folly	47
Ardale Community Home	17
Arden Hall	53
Aveley Marshes	5
Aveley	5ff
Baker Street Windmill	50
Bata Estate	40
Beacon Hill	13
Belhus	7,8
Belmont Castle	20
Benton's Farm	9
Birch Cottage	47
Bishop Bonner's Palace	48
Blackshots Wildlife Area	20
Botany Bay Gardens	12
Bothy, The	46
Bulphan	46ff
Chadwell Place	27
Churches - see Subjects/Groups index	
Civic Hall	20
Civic Offices	22
Coal Road	35
Coalhouse Fort	38
Condovers	37
Conway's Farm	46
Coppid Hall	10,19
Corringham	67ff
Corringham Light Railway	67
Coryton	67
Dartford Tunnel	13
Davy Down	10,17
Dell, The	24

80

Deneholes	25,26
Dipping, The	12
Dunton	55
Duvals	20
East Tilbury Battery	37
Fisher's Farm	71
Fobbing	68ff
Fobbing Marsh	71
Ford Place	17
Garrison Estate	12
Grays	20ff
Grays Beach	23
Grays Co-Op.	22
Grays Hall	10,24
Grays Library	22,45
Grays Wharf	23
Great Malgraves	53
Great Garlands	66
Groves Manor	11
Hassingbrook	64
Hastings	15
Heath Place	43
High House	13
Horndon-on-the-Hill	55ff
Horndon Penny	55
Horndon Mill	55
Inns - see Subjects/Groups index	
Ivy Walls	65
Kenningtons	5
Kynochtown	67
Lakeside	14
Langdon Hills	53,54
Larkin's Corner	46
Linford	61
Little Belhus	8
Loft Hall	44
Lorkins Farm	46
Low Street	37

Maltings	6,46
Mardyke	17
Marshall's	35
Mill House	5,34
Moore Place	65
Mucking	62ff
New Jenkyns	63
North Stifford	17ff
Old Hall Farmhouse	48
One Tree Hill	54
Orsett	44ff
Orsett Academy	49
Orsett Hall	44
Orsett Heath	44
Orsett Hospital	49
Orsett House	49
Oxford Medical Mission	55
Palmer's School	15,19,23,25
Plotlands, The	53
Polwicks	37
Potash Hill	44
Powder Magazines	11,12
Pumping Station	17
Purfleet	11ff
Purfleet Rifle Range	5
Queen Elizabeth II Bridge	13
Quince Tree House	9
Red Hills	40
Saffron Gardens	58,59
Shellhaven	66
Slades Hold	49
Sleeper's Farm	28
South Ockendon	8ff
South Ockendon Hall	10
South Ockendon Hospital	9
South Ockendon Windmill	10,17
South Stifford	20ff

St. Clere's Hall	61
Stanford-le-Hope	63ff
Stanford Warren	63
State Cinema	22
Stuart Estate	23,24
Thames Chase	11,17
Thameshaven	66
Thurrock	2,31
Thurrock College	27
Thurrock Community Hospital	20
Tilbury	31ff
Tilbury Docks	31
Tilbury Environment Centre	34
Tilbury Fort	33,43
Tilbury Power Station	33
Tilbury-Gravesend Ferry	32
Vange Wells	54
Vineyard, The	69
Walton's Hall	61
Watts Wood	11
West Thurrock	14ff,20
West Thurrock Power Station	14
West Tilbury	34ff
West Tilbury Wells	36
Wheeler's	71
Whitechapel Charity	38
Whitecrofts	43
William Edwards School	19
Woolmarket, The	57
Zlin	40

Subjects/Groups Index

Archaeology 26,49,53,62
Armada Site 34
Artists/Craftsmen -
    Ashbee, Charles Robert 56,59
    Chapman & Andre 9,34,46
    Comper 47
    Connolly H.C. 27
    Coode-Adams B.R. 68
    Corbusier, Le 40
    Cox A. 21
    Frith 43
    Heskett, Phillipa 23
    Lloyd Wright, Frank 40
    Nicholson, Sir Charles 25,47
    Ogilby & Morgan 58
    Oldfield, William 39
    Smith, Ray 21
    Turner, Thomas 45
    Walker, John 34,36
    Warburton, John 58

Aveley Elephants 5
Boundary/Charity posts 20,24,26,35,38,68
Churches -
    All Saints, Grays 25
    All Saints, Langdon Hills 54
    Congregational, Orsett 47
    Evangelical, Stanford-le-Hope 64
    Lodge Lane Methodist, Grays 20
    St. Clement, West Thurrock 14,15,17,62
    St. Giles & All Saints, Orsett 47
    St. James, West Tilbury 36
    St. John the Baptist, Mucking 62
    St. Katherine, East Tilbury 38
    St. Margaret of Antioch, Stanford 64

St. Mary, Bulphan	46
St. Mary, Chadwell	27
St. Mary, Corringham	67
St. Mary, Little Thurrock	26
St. Mary, North Stifford	18
St. Michael, Aveley	6
St. Michael, Fobbing	69
St. Michael, Pitsea	14
St. Nicholas, South Ockendon	9,10
St. Peter & St. Paul, Grays	22,23
St. Peter & St. Paul, Horndon	56
St. Runwald, Colchester	14
St. Stephen, Purfleet	12
Wesleyan Methodist, South Ockendon	10

Companies -
Anglo-Saxon Petroleum Co.	66
Aveley Methane Ltd.	5
Bata Co.	40
Blue Circle Ltd.	13
Cory Bros.	67
Kynoch & Co.	67
London & Thameshaven Oil Wharves Ltd.	66
Miners' Safety Explosive Co.	66
Mobil Oil Co.	67
Procter & Gamble Ltd.	14
Shell Co.	66
Vacuum Oil Co.	67
Van den Bergh Foods Ltd.	13
White Horse Ferries Ltd.	32

Heraldry	8,19,23,31,38,39,45, 46,47,50,59,64,69

Inns -
Bell	57,58
Blue Anchor	35
Bricklayers	12

Bull	27
Crown	48,63
Crown & Anchor	6
Dog & Partridge	17,45
Dog & Gun	47
Five Bells	71
Foxhound	48
Harrow	17
Hoy	23
Jolly Sailor	21
King's Arms	50
Knight of Aveley	7
Lennards	5
Plough House Motel	45
Queen Victoria Temperance Hotel	22
Queen's Hotel	21
Royal Oak	9,10
Royal Hotel	12
Sailor's Return	21
Ship	12,69
Sir Henry Gurnet	5
Stifford Moathouse	19
Theobald Arms	23
Wharf	21
White Lion	69
Whitmore Arms	47
Wingrove's Hotel	12
World's End	32

Kings & Queens -

Anne	39
Charles I	24
Charles II	24,33
Edward the Confessor	55
Edward VII	12
Elizabeth I	34,59,69
Elizabeth II	13

Frederick II	63
George I	46
George II	19,61
George III	10,12,39,58
George IV	69
George V	20
George VI	44
Henry III	63
Henry VII	10
Henry VIII	33,69
Richard (Coeur-de-Lion)	21
Richard III	10
Victoria	22,43

Orsett Show	45
Peasants' Revolt	68
Place Name Origins	2,6,11,21,27,36,46, 55,61,62,63,64,66,67
Street Names	6,8,9,11,19,20,23,24, 26,31,35,40,61,64
Thurrock Museum	5,8,35,38,43,67

Writers -

Andree, Dr. J.	36
Bede, The Venerable	36
Brooks, Herbert	19
Conrad, Joseph	65,66
Defoe, Daniel	32
Dickens, Charles	66
Diehl, Alice	8
Eliot T.S.	21
Foxe	56
Macaulay	35
Palin, Rev. Wm.	18,19,63
Pepys, Samuel	14
Pevsner	14
Randall, Martha	43

Sheridan	33
Stephenson, Rev. Samuel	67
Stoker, Bram	13
Tilbury, Gervaise de	37
Wallace, Alfred Russell	24
Whitton, Charles	27
Williams, Col. R.H.	37
Young, Arthur	53,54